NEW YORK REVIEW BOOKS
POETS

GLORIA GERVITZ was born in Mexico City into an Eastern European Jewish immigrant family. She was awarded the Pablo Neruda Prize for Poetry in 2019. Her main body of work is *Migraciones*, a single poem that evolved organically over forty-four years. Gervitz has translated poetry by Samuel Beckett, Kenneth Rexroth, Lorine Niedecker, Susan Howe, and Rita Dove into Spanish. She now lives in San Diego, California.

MARK SCHAFER is a literary translator, a visual artist, and a senior lecturer at the University of Massachusetts Boston, where he teaches Spanish. He has translated works by authors from around the Spanish-speaking world, including David Huerta, Belén Gopegui, Virgilio Piñera, and Alberto Ruy Sánchez. Schafer is a founding member of the Boston Area Literary Translators Group. He lives in Roxbury, Massachusetts, the traditional and unceded territory of the Massachusett and Wampanoag Peoples.

T0018956

Gloria Gervitz

Migrations
Poem, 1976—2020

TRANSLATED FROM THE SPANISH
BY MARK SCHAFER

NYRB/POETS

 NEW YORK REVIEW BOOKS   *New York*

THIS IS A NEW YORK REVIEW BOOK
PUBLISHED BY THE NEW YORK REVIEW OF BOOKS
435 Hudson Street, New York, NY 10014
www.nyrb.com

Library of Congress Cataloging-in-Publication Data
Names: Gervitz, Gloria, 1943– author. | Schafer, Mark, translator.
Title: Migrations: poem, 1976–2020 / by Gloria Gervitz; translated by Mark
 Schafer.
Other titles: Migraciones. English
Description: New York: New York Review Books, [2021] | Series: New York
 Review Books poets
Identifiers: LCCN 2021012386 (print) | LCCN 2021012387 (ebook) |
 ISBN 9781681375700 (paperback) | ISBN 9781681375717 (ebook)
Subjects: LCGFT: Poetry.
Classification: LCC PQ7298.17.E755 M5413 2021 (print) | LCC PQ7298.17.E755
 (ebook) | DDC 861/.64—dc23
LC record available at https://lccn.loc.gov/2021012386
LC ebook record available at https://lccn.loc.gov/2021012387

ISBN 978-1-68137-570-0
Available as an electronic book; ISBN 978-1-68137-571-7

Cover and book design by Emily Singer

Printed in the United States of America on acid-free paper.
10 9 8 7 6 5 4 3 2 1

Contents

Migrations

in the migrations of red carnations where songs burst from long-beaked birds
and apples rot before the disaster
where women fondle their breasts and touch their sex
in the sweat of rice powder and teatime
vines of passionflowers course through that which stays the same
cities crisscrossed by thought
Ash Wednesday
the old nanny watches us from a shaft of light
pools of shadow breathe
purples rain down nearly red
the heat opens its jaws
the moon sinks into the street and the voice of a black woman
a sad black woman sings and swells
incense of gladioli
and your fingers slip inside me like warm mollusks
we're in the brittleness of autumn's hide
in the rectangular park
in the dog days of summer
when the lightest colors are most deeply moving
after Shaharit
raw appeals now forgotten
winds rise lightly rinsed by prayer
forest of pepper trees
and my grandmother always played the same sonata

a girl eats a snow cone in Chapultepec
the ivy vine tangles in the mist
the light splinters
and the clothes hang in the sun
my grandmother's sonata is impenetrable
you said it was summertime oh music
and the invasion of dawns
and the invasion of greens
down below shouts of children at play
vendors of nuts
breath of yellow roses
and as we left the movies my grandmother told me
dream that the dream of life is beautiful my child
beneath the summer-drenched willow only restlessness lingers
docile clouds descend into silence
the day dissolves in the hot air
green erupts within green
I spread my legs beneath the bathtub faucet
gushing water falls
the water enters me
the words of the Zohar spread open
the same questions as always
and I sink deeper and deeper
in the vertigo of Kol Nidre
before the start of the great fast
in the blue haze of the synagogues
after and before Rosh Hashanah
in the whiteness of the rain
my grandmother prays the rosary
and in the background plummeting
the echo of the shofar opens the year
into the gulf of absences to the northeast
pour words saliva
insomnias

and farther to the east
I masturbate thinking of you
the screech of seagulls the break of day
the froth in the dazzle of the wing
the color and the season of bougainvilleas are for you
the pollen still on my fingers
your scent of violets sour and feverish from the dust
words that are nothing but a drawn-out prayer
a form of madness after the madness
the cages where the perfumes are shut away
the endless delights
the voluptuousness of being born again and again
static ecstasy
move
more even more
don't be afraid
and the photographs fading in the fermentation of silence
the unscreened porches
fever growing red in other skies
the gleaming verandas darkening with the acacias
and in the kitchen the newly washed dishes
fruit and syrups
in the swell of rivers
in the night of willows
in the washbasins of dreams
in that steam of female viscera
rising unmistakable and expansive
I leave you my death entire complete
my whole death for you
to whom does one speak before dying?
where are you?
where in me can I invent you?
and the milagros piling up in the church of Santa Clara
and the atrium filling with tears

ink flowers in spent Hebrew
dripping from the Torah scrolls
skidding slowly
the days slipping away
squeezed by my migraine
I can't find myself
I don't even have candles for my wake
I don't even know the words of the Kaddish
I've lost my bearings
where does the beating break?
how can I cast off this last shred of sleep?
and the house lashed to a tree lashed to the wind
the leaves and their opal shadow
spiral of echoes
reverberation
we are what we think
the thought behind the thought
the cranes return
spread silence with their wings
sudden white flowers in an empty sky
in the cities at noon
farther and farther south
when heat surrounds the mountains' breath
always to the south
I prefer to cling to my inventions
and not to know what really exists
better to dream that I'm dead
and not to die of all the dreams that invent me
I go back to sleep and dream no more
and the light stumbling on the brink of day
and the cry of the trees a deafening roar
and the afternoon just repeats itself
doesn't disclose that lull in reality
the only inhabitable place

fleeting geometry
slow shuttered insomnia
dawn draining away
a sun of bees breaking apart
and as my grandmother prays her rosary it rains
and as they say Kaddish for me it rains
and I'm more distant by the day and don't know what to do
I can't escape myself
and only know and feel others inside me
an invention that starts up every morning
the tedious learning to wake up and become myself again
and if I woke up once and for all?
the morning melts away
intervals of warm silence
sharpened spaces
sudden structures
rectangles
I can see fragments almost smells
each level has its own blood flow
my nanny accompanies me as I pack my things to go
doves all around the room flapping of wings
I open the window
minute fissures ache atrophy
inflame the afternoon
I can't feel what I am
I am what I was
and what I wish to be
in the soaring of orchids centers open to penetration
on the perimeter
girlfriends lightly caressing themselves
because it's always the first time
because we've been born again and again
and always return
and the flowers opening

and the high birds oh so high pausing in flight
shredding themselves on the clouds
and the rained-out clouds filling with wings
in the span of the dream
I wake and it's almost nighttime
I walk into a movie theater
it's snowing in New York
I walk into another
the present is just a circumstance
I descend
it's almost eight in the morning
and it's January
we elapse within ourselves
I'm living overlapping moments flattened on a plane
I spread over afternoons that exist for me alone
outside the windows are today's hours
I don't know this day
I cling to my other days
cling to myself
hang on to myself
and even so even so everything comes to an end
even those things for all time come to an end
even old habits come to an end in the end
small saturated moments swell
merge in their dissolution
though I remain shut away in this room
though it keeps on raining
though I still can feel that I can feel
though it still makes me keep on feeling
and fear makes me break out of fear
and I make myself break out of myself
but why believe all this when across the ocean
geraniums bloom all year long
and large trunks laden with warm resinous odors

overflow in unfamiliar bedrooms
and ointments and soaps made of oats and goat milk
face powder made of wheat toothpaste that tastes of chewing gum
and those rinses for untangling hair on drawn-out days
Venetian blinds scorched by the green sun of Cuernavaca
a girl gazes at her sex in the heat of midday
thick with insects and lizards
I'm not sure whether to sleep is to be awake
my hands get in my way I don't know where to put them
the slow rain almost stops
everything stops grips me but the rain falls
windows open
below them dunes
and farther still ships set sail like an exhalation
bound for the girls in the frescoes at the palace of Knossos
girls of water and lime
and the skin sloughs off
and underneath a dusty sun
and farther in birds
and we never get farther than ourselves
but all year long geraniums bloom in distant memory
and the green blinds are there in that memory as well
beats etching themselves on a daguerreotype
where are they beating?
where are they?
something slides heads toward cessation
I'm far from the mornings
far from men and women
far from habits and customs
I let myself fall
the sky clouds over
the irretrievable yellow
the soft fall
colors lost

shattering
tenacity of white
and the first words of the Torah are inscribed
in the atonement of white
in the anguish of white
in the neutrality of white
I'm hanging on to life
gusts of sun
gusting rain
nearly blue ramifications
hair a mess and that smell
that smell rising from childhood
a lingering streak of yellow
flutters reappears
now sways gently
from a distance it almost looks like a sketch of a sunflower
now it uncouples barely discernible against the white
once more it pierces the substance of nothingness
once more the dreams start clinging to that almost still-yellow streak
I'm not going anywhere everything is here here is there
I identify intensely with the dust
sharp shifting empty vast landscape
I can't ford the air
I start to live off the breeze
I wish I could pray and don't know how
I don't even know what I want to say
everything is inundated
there are no edges
there is quietude
there is all I don't understand
and I did not invent that girl
she thrust her existence inside me
darkest roses sprouting in memory
the women braiding their hair scenting their armpits

the smell of sex ripening
and in the Jewish quarters high and low hidden in the mornings of Segovia
the love affairs of Jewish girls and Christian noblemen
still stalk the bridges
and the tales of the Haggadah proliferating
as I wait bleary-eyed in airport lobbies
in landscapes of neurons nearly on the threshold of the oracle of Delphi
there is one and only one answer
no explanation is forthcoming
barely the incision
and my mother and some friends play bridge
and chain-smoke cigarettes
and the women's perfume mingled with the white
grows dark
through the windows the nearly forgotten pepper trees
pale wind
whiff of wicker on the faded porch
the house dissolves
eternity of the gardens of sand
doggedness of the wind
the leaves curl begin their return
I wake up and the girlfriends tremble in the willows
the shady veranda cool in the bustle of linen
I brush your brown hair
we barely move
pollen coats that distant memory of mirrors
it still burns I touch myself I'm alone
dawns from the other floods
beloved distant one
complicity of the voice
its persistence
and I am what is falling
now I'm in a landscape full of mockingbirds
I get closer and closer

when I claim that vastness
I'll barely have the strength to wake in the brevity of death
the light strikes the air
we're in the place where the colors open
the days are long and clench like migraines
and everything repeats
the trees casting off
the night dissolving
and then?
nothing is true but the reflection of the dream I'm trying to shatter
and which I don't even dare to dream
constant plagiarism of myself
and time is the only meeting place
it's all nothing but time
there where a few sprigs of bougainvillea in a glass of water
suffice to make us a garden
because we die alone
and death is just the awakening
from this first dream of living
and my grandmother said as we left the movies
dream that the dream of life is beautiful my child
the candles' glow grows rusty
and I where am I?
I'm who I always was
the surprise of being
I come to where everything starts the beginning of the beginning
this is the time
the time for waking up
my grandmother lights the Shabbos candles from her death and looks at me
Shabbat lengthens into never into after into before
my grandmother who died of dreams
endlessly rocks the dream that invents her
which I invent

a wild girl looks at me from inside

I am whole

and the weavers of wicker chairs came
and the carpenters with their boards of oak and orangewood
and the blacksmiths with railings like climbing vines
and the men selling plants and the scatterbrained joiners
and at the end of the brick porch the orchids and the cages of canaries
the cardinal and the budgie and the gardenias awash in perfume
                                        and that zest for life

they rinse my hair with water from a gourd and turn up the radio
and I smell of Palmolive and roses happiness is strewn around and the
    mother sings boleros

they prepare the room for the ritual bath
the walls are daubed with almond oil
the thick shine of the mosaics and the submerged ledges
and the women waxing their legs coo like doves
in the white eucalyptus steam

clouds red as veins plow the afternoon
tides turn
break day break

they've slathered me with spikenard
and basil

they hold me up for I'm reeling
they put me to sleep in a purple sky

standing on the bamboo mat
I wash my vulva clitoris hard and full

and my pleasure grows so intense
that I even pee on myself

I feel vulnerable with short hair
                    where am I returning?
I'm anchored
          absence of dust
                         the stillness of objects
is utterly quietly motionless within me

                                   in another memory
                    transparency of the unfathomable
the lace curtains parting
                         a woman a window

the trees wings crashing in the light
                              and the woman in the window

                         the scene after whiteness

the telephones in the offices are busy and the secretaries
type the same memo again and again and don't know they're alive

which portion of reality is most fragile
                                        mine
          or the one in which others see me?

and the plummeting music
and the photographs in cigar boxes

the wires thin as threads rivers of swallows
the heat like a boar's tusk

the sun plunging into the dog days of summer
and she a bunch of calla lilies in her arm stepping ashore at the Port of
    Veracruz

do you remember?

break memory
break me

sprawled on the wicker armchair before the mirror legs spread open
she takes pleasure in her body

far from the oracle clutching the orchids' depth she can taste the arrival of
    pleasure
and in reverie she strokes her vulva with saliva-slick fingers

who is that woman who overflows me drowning in herself?
and I never tire of hearing the songs of Bola de Nieve over and over and over
    again

and the blue after mass at the breaking of day and the passionflower vines of
    rain
as if nothing at all had happened

and my nanny tugs at my freshly washed hair and braids it with worsted
    ribbons
and the smell of coffee rises

                                            why did you wake me?

and it doesn't rain
and I saw myself in the real reality
the invulnerable drought and the beasts and the sunrise

                                                palm trees
                                                        distances
                                am I scared?

imagination what we dreamt now irreversible begun again and always far away
                                                                    recollections

and we weren't there and it's summertime grazed by oxen and all is still
                                            the old house in its midst
                                the roses opening to the exuberance of oblivion

        and I unwilling to enter those rooms
                with nothing but the sound of my breath

                        a cloud scuds by   shadow of a hummingbird

            where was I all this time?

                                    why doesn't it rain?

and it doesn't rain
and the willows leaning
and the light shedding its leaves
        and my life more planned than lived
                is there still time?

in the instability of other memories the hired mourners keen
in the dog-day heat puddles of clay planters and the glare of the sun

we girls would walk upstream
yellow baskets full of soap plant for scrubbing clothes
we'd pound the morning with stones
lye in the hollow
acrid crystal clear
trickling
spreading its branches
blossoming
scattering me inward

where would I go if I could get there?   what would I be if I went?

                can you hear me?

drink me as though I were water
                    pour me out

and hiding in the broad sweep of the dress
                              sinking
                    shy
                                   a scent the color of lilac
                                   a petal

the petals barely covering her
          the lilacs unraveling between her legs

               desire monotonous and black like a gleaming lacquered box

     and like a perfume grown old in the bottle
she didn't look like anyone
                              couldn't even remember

                    what should I remember?

                    what forgotten fear should I remember?

and the words talk
          and talk

     and talk

     and I don't want to hear them   don't want to
                        and I do

                          and fear bolting
and the basket full of unwashed clothes
     and the memories piling up

and I cloistering myself like a nun
     encasing myself in thick coarse cloth

hiding from my body
     hiding from myself

the absence of desire is as intense as passion
     the absence of desire in her body makes her cry out

            the rain starts to fall   it's barely rain
                    it's helplessness

                      a wrenching apart

my dead are as real as I am and I speak to them in Russian and Yiddish

and in the house the gleaming floor tiles
the darkness growing damp in the wardrobes
the starched linen sheets
the impeccable clothing that still holds your scent
and the dust hiding like an animal

and you why do you hide behind a migraine when I speak to you?

do you hear me?

do you hear me?

you were always the most beautiful
no one else mattered
                              oh maleficent one
banish me
let me leave
take pity on me
you who have given me comfort
help me forget you

do you hear me?
are you still here with me?
                              could it be that you're my echo?

I'm in the very place
the very place where everything began
where it begins
where it all begins
nearly forgotten
she the same girl
though barely if still yet a girl

I open the blinds and close the blinds
and the table is set and the table is cleared
and I turn the lights on and turn them off
and I fold the clothes and unfold and fold
and the same dust and the same long dry season
and the empty bottles refilled should you come
and the wind falls
and the leaves fall
and I fall

rock me
        swaddle me

        and if one day you aren't there to reply?
                and if you don't come?

and if you leave these bedrooms that I dust for you never to return?

                        and all this does it matter?

you're hurting me
        let go of me
        don't take what I've learned on my own

the women sit on the floor
        I say Kaddish for you and for me
the words are worn like the marble of those pietàs worn by kisses
                Mother of God pray for us

and she who came from Kiev
a bunch of flowers clasped to her bosom
a life meant to be lived in a more expansive time
oh mother whom I forgot
now and at the hour of our death
Adonai Eloheinu Adonai Echad
farewell
farewell
oh mother
farewell

                    and who cares about these memories?

she a girl with flowers
and her pleated dresses and her bright red mouth smiling
now just a photograph stored in a cigar box

she and the midday sun
white flowers
and her two children clutching her skirt
strolling through Mexico Park

she who didn't know the Kaddish
bidding farewell in a train station
bidding farewell to parents brothers sisters
she would never see again

she
oh so many dreams that never reached the sea

she fat
old before her time
                    how could this have happened to me?
hair pulled back
and the look of a wounded animal

and you were distant from the others
and you were distant from yourself
and the taste of tea from that samovar in your house
                              stayed with you forever

do you hear my sobbing?
do you hear my sobbing covering you like cloth?
tear it apart
break me
cover me with your ashes
set me free

I await the night like a tethered animal stamping
                                        stamping
and I accuse you
and what can I blame you for
                    how could it have been otherwise?

the oracle is fulfilled

let me leave
let go of me
don't return
I don't want to stay here trapped in your dream unable to wake up
                                        which way?

I make it no farther than the place of beginnings
return to kiss your wrist
to fall on my knees
devoutly I kiss the veins of your hands
oh mother have mercy on me
oh merciful mother
have mercy on me
uphold me
vanquish me but give me comfort

I rest my head
touch your heart
close my eyes
I'm a girl lashed to you like the drowned man is
to the stone tied around his neck

                    I'm no longer afraid
I can sink no farther beneath your heart

take the light
            night

                    without putting up a fight
in the waiting
                in the annunciation
in the stillness that precedes the visitation
                            that precedes the name
in the sheer beauty of return
                    in the fever
in the obliterated perception
                    in the fragility
no one to tell this to
                who can tell her own life?

and there wasn't time for I'd been waiting for something else another word
the unspoken one the one unheard

                            and we scattered in the daily routine

and the words we never said the true ones the ones that truly said something
remained in that dream from which we couldn't wake
                                listen to them

            now that you're no longer here let me tell you

and spawning into infinitesimal stars
dawn
and the white fading in the furniture and in her clothes
and in the petals
and in the roses

and the body withering
and smelling of urine

and the girl who cried as she clasped her dead mother
is still crying inside me

I move close to the silence now

was it you who opened the window?
that one I was looking for is me
there's no proof

just the slightest breathing of an old woman far away
me
the wrinkled nightgown
the endless day
the still air
calmness in a straight line
white beating on white
the pulse slower and slower
slowly
I clench release clench
breathe   breathe
I'm breathing myself
I'm breathing
breathing
and who will remember me?

murmur of arteries
                              just breathing
she barely breathing as on any given day

                                        a memory passes through
crickets on the edge of the afternoon
                              no nights

        I sleep in memory

                              open my eyes

        nothing
                        no one
        me   still me
                        אבר המש שדקתיו לדגתי

I'm farther away
                can you see me?

I want to wake up

for now my hands and feet stay right where they are
I fold my nightgown and put it away

                              why not open my eyes in the darkness
                              in darkness itself as in the beginning

then I opened the window

יזכר אלהים נשמת אמי מורתי שהלכה לעולמה

one will die alone   alone in the dark
far from what one was or imagined oneself to be

one dies in the most ordinary of feelings
the enormous surprise that one is dying

one burrows into the darkness
and lies down there like an animal

like Jonah in the belly of the whale
like the sibyl within the dank walls
not knowing what to say with nothing to say
for you always yours
this faithfulness must have been to myself

old feelings carefully forgotten shatter oblivion
and you know I speak to you no one but you always to you

the air fills with flowers
the rain shifts toward dream as well
slowly reclaims its shadow
leans like a willow
                        falls
I return home

do you hear me? here I am under my name
the forgotten little girl says she doesn't know says she doesn't know
                                    she-wolf are you there?

and to remember myself I return to you
how alone you must feel
        (this is just the testimony of one who listens)

                              are you listening to me?

abase me memory that I might offer forgiveness
who could speak words of compassion?
                              stay here

February
I speak of those times living in themselves
I see that face once more
        can I ever yank myself from myself?

I listen through underground walls to the prisoners
sending signals to one another

                      memory do you hear me?
you grow like all that is forgotten

and the woman I am
offers forgiveness to the one I once was

some photographs on the table
that girl the one in the front on the left
                                yes that's me

witness   answer

                    answer me

the voice

       falls

            the words fall

and what is born of them falls

     don't explain   lost in you

                   is you

     don't explain   every year

              Yizkor

she cries
without touching her I cry with her involuntarily
reach for the place of her heart

our sobbing is lost in the darkness of sleep in the dark of night
in the darkness of the house in the dullness of silence
we're the ones who leave

she watches her continues watching eyes closed
I wish I could wake up and talk to you but I have nothing to say

and thirty days after your death standing before that mound of earth and
    stones one hears
that song the men of the desert sing
                      though you don't know Aramaic
                                listen to it

I clear off the stones so the words can penetrate

the woman framed by her own landscape leaning on the railing
the waves in that ostensible stillness hold fast her dream
and bursting abrupt into the dream the words of the Kaddish
and the men playing dominoes and drinking beer
and the boy sleeping and the afternoon sinking
and at the railing the shape of her body
(reverberation of her gray dress)

a girl alone on the pier
the heat is very intense the light is white and wounds
the light is so violent it strips her bare
plunders her
the light is endless she has to close her eyes
the boy lets go of her hand
she's there for the first time and forever
the light is emptied
I descend
through closed blinds music I've never heard before
I descend
peddlers selling unfamiliar fruit
I descend
long endless descent

the same scene over again

the woman on the pier dazzled
the boy races around the promenade
the longing forever within her
beyond the sea the other edge of nostalgia
I was unfair to my mother
and after all what did I do with my life?
I descend

we went ashore one day at noon at the Port of Veracruz
we were wearing our grandparents' lambswool coats
and in Havana I ate nisperos and mangoes for the first time
                                    who can I tell this to?

memory of the sea and its tedium
of the girl I was then
of the dress that now looks ridiculous in the photograph

memory of the mottled planks of the ship
of those fearless waves in all their beauty
memory of the almost unbearable moon

and it's noon and it's today and I go ashore and it's a day in August
and I'd never clung so fiercely to life

she would die across the sea that's the only thing she's sure of
what once was what never will be again

none of what disturbed her can be seen in that photograph taken before she left
hair pulled back and the boy by her side in those flat passport pictures

she is real only as far as I can imagine her

would we have been friends?

she looks at me she says she wishes she would die
(it's not true she's so full of joy which is why she thinks of death)
I carefully set aside the memories that bind me to that heart

and she yanks herself from her shadow and the words can't reach her
and life is the only refuge and you you died on me you died on me in me

and the earth thaws and I can't say why this morning will stay with me forever
it's the smell of irises filtering through the snow
(actually it's a morning like any other)
why is this the one I keep?

stubborn dreams gifts for no one barely for herself
the photograph doesn't reveal a thing (she's still a young woman)
                                        I never knew her

            when exactly did those dreams begin to haunt me?

the cry comes without tears voiceless stripped bare
it's as close as I can get
she doesn't want me to remember her
                              let me talk
and the far-off cry
and the words could not touch her heart
                              roses on the last step

and once again I don't recognize the voice

that girl standing alone on the pier
                          this fixed image
            what life was this?

                  and what does all this mean?

                              and my voice mingling with yours
                    the birds thrashing against the light

summer spilling over
and she writing letters in a Yiddish no one speaks anymore

                                    am I that woman?

I walk to the railing look at the sea I don't recall a thing
nothing to cling to

and all those people where are they now?

nothing you say nothing to me
    nothing there's nothing left

        the tedium of waiting
the diagram of the rain   the sinking of dreams

and I'm ashamed of my foreign accent
      and the customs of my family

perhaps we're the same darkness the same words the same cries
you'll never know the dead don't understand the living

and if I approached your open jaws and if I approached remorse
you who no longer listen to me you who no longer hear me cry

offer me forgiveness gather me into your indifference
the earth has undone you you don't know I'm here

the rain grows stronger we're complicit
                              grant me your oblivion

                                        now where is your death?

and that smell of wet wood
that damp briny smell

under the light the withered women (many in wigs)
murmur newly learned words in that foreign tongue

repeat them like a litany
the stars unhitch themselves from the night

continue on their way
I trail them blindly from where I stand

I still hear the fog-draped sirens' song
still know nothing of forgetting nor of forgiveness

and what were you seeking in that dream?
give me longing that I might seek you
everything I've loved disappeared
I'm besieged
pray for me

I search the damp earth for a place to die
how do I find you?

the rain falls
                    fulfills
watching it is not to insist

        from there back to the beginning

I kiss these edges doubt
the habit of waking remains

                morning
the momentary flowers

            who will remember my house?

feeling was not enough
even serenity wasn't enough

my life left no trace
                water on water
                    lackluster

for years I've spoken in a language not my own
                                could it be I'm ready to die?

how can I hold on to you?
I fill my hands with those irises plucked from the snow

                           the irises wither

                                  return to the earth

who knows if we'll ever meet again

I'll never know I don't know if you can hear me

                                  what do the dead remember?

outside the rain falls silent

                                                (bless me mother)

I'm very close to your heart do you hear me?

                                                       darkness spreads

the time we have to live is so short

I fall in the dream without leaving the dream

                                           it's a day like any other

                                                 outside it rains

the willows loosen themselves from the rain
so much time has passed since I was here last

                    don't judge me mother
you too are doomed to be forgotten

the rain stopped only its shadow remains
the voices nearly slip through
                              the same ones?
I don't know

will you let me be alone with myself one day?
will you let me become who I am one day?

                                   will you let me?

then I had the dream or the visitation of the dream
I feel restless like the traveler before arrival
I want to understand or wake up
the water sparkles like a knife
                    it was the Lethe

as if I were nostalgic for the one I am now
                                nostalgic for myself
as if I could begin again
as if I'd moved to another house
as if I were repeating words that are mantras
as if it were a monologue you say to yourself
as if I were the one who's begun to die and not you
as if fear and dust were one

morning made of clay
morning made of rivers

and memories are the bridge
where to?   where from?

a trail of light remains with no more substance than an idea
the sun like a bullet in the crevice of the day

                      and in the room your dream
deep and sweet like a beloved animal

I don't have the place just the longing for the place the routine
and the passing time

I follow the dream's movement its infinitesimal traces
       I follow the river's movement its weight its particles
                              its silence its larvae its labyrinths
       stars that float like husks

                   the morning's left
                          the forgotten one
            the morning for keeping out of sight
            the morning for weeping
                          the dense the dreaded
                                   the long
                                   the indefinable
                          the quiet morning

                   and the air an arc curving under the acacias

I've built my dreams near the rocks
chose this parched landscape

                              this perseverance this thirst
nothing sadder than this immensity that is little more than nothing

the stone is troubled by its dreams

perhaps its transparency
is time in a different darkness

how can I hold on to you?

in the old house (now a restaurant)
with its mottled floor tiles and high ceilings?

in the gardens of stone and sand seen so many years ago?

in my fear?

come tell me
>do you see me in you?
>>do you see me?

come forgotten one
come and flood me with tears
flood me with tears that I might lament you
I'll touch your lucidity and the flotsam of this day
I'll lick your hands like an animal
look at me
>don't disappear
>>don't leave me

come sobbed one

dissolve me on your tongue like a host
        unto the greediness of dust

    don't leave me

let me in you let me be in you let me ache in you
let me weep in you
          don't leave me

drag me to the breach of the day
leave me in its stillness
in its coarseness

and the water in its silence of roots
in its slowness of roots
opens itself trembling

and the morning groans
and sways with the old words
the long the sunken words

give them to me that I might seek you give them to me
that I might open myself not to the knowledge of you
but to the muddled premonition of the path that leads to you

I speak to you from those words
from thought and the idea of thought
from you and the beginning that emanates from you
from the desire to reach you

and morning breaks
and Shaharit begins
        oh splendorous splendorous
    splendorous

listen to me
wherever you might be
listen to me

there's a dizziness in this light
and the day plummets
and swallows pierce the moment

what do the gods know of the dreams of men?

it's in this light that I'm consumed
in its transparency
where I seek you most

it's in the parched expanse of this morning
imperceptible spilled
water on the lips of the thirsty

mother I'm the one I seek
I've carried you on my back
feeling your weight

and oblivion aches in me
like a wound
the light hushes

and I heard you inside me
heard you at the breach
being born

and the words sank
and the cry soaked into the sand
and I stood on the edge

and there was something beloved in the days and in the memory of the days
and it took me my whole life to wake up
but we never said what mattered most

it was near the dark heart of the willows
where I still invoke your name and prostrate myself before you
as before as always

I stand beneath a pale sky
always the enormous pale silence
and it dwelled in me like a blossoming

waking up on the other side
and I wanted to know
but was only allowed to ask

autumn draws taut as a bow
the rain also glides toward sleep
gradually regains its shadow

leans like a willow
               falls

waves of light swell upward
                        wailing

in the vast stillness of the name
the pierced word
wandering mortal and alone

feeling her way
the priestess
complicit old mother

intercedes

oh summoned one
              night dweller
          like a pool of fear

opening in your hunger
you rivet your widow's eyes
on the arduousness of love

          and night
every branch trembling
kneels at the abyss
covers me like a tear

and we tumble together down the slope
complicit

open me with your saliva
plunge to my depths   to my desolation

receive me as if I were a fistful of dirt

                             the passage itself

the words
brief   moist

brush the surface
like a snake

and the voice knows it doesn't know

avalanche of leaves
and their brittle red lament

the river bends
to its thirst
       time moves more quickly than I do

the night breaks off
I touch the waters of its nakedness
           and she cries out within the cry

I entered the place entered an orphan

where are the words why don't they appear?
why don't they come to my aid?

suddenly
   light

water like a scourge
left tunneling in its violence

and I have no voice to tell it

between the walls
      your cries

      knot
        spiral

        edge

and the stone in its dream
in its clay

          plummeting
     to the bottom of itself

and the pounding voice
deaf
          capsizing
     in the empty sky

and they sowed the fields with salt
and plowed them with salt
and the scribe sealed the words

in the cleansing of the quarry
faith in its labyrinth
                in its rending apart

and she
full of longing   prostrate

and alone at the bottom of herself
                              larva

she shudders
contracts like a mollusk
                    pale

              stalking
in her innermost depths

darkest dilation

in the abyss of its water
the spring sheds light on itself

overflowing
ear strained
        anchor

and you   and you

she floats in the belly of the earth
facedown like a suicide

touch me inside you
with that overflowing restraint

touch me
in this dark place of thought

in my unfathomability
in that other unfathomable me

                    ah if only you could tattoo me
if only you'd stayed there
if you'd only stayed

like a blind bitch
giving suck

stay
give me the words

I ought to uproot you
trample you down

frail
trembling

reconcile me with myself
that the earth might weigh lightly on me

I don't know how to go on
I am dry

I speak for you speak from you
and pain sliding down like a drop of water

damp ideograms
illegible strokes
on this spring equinox

the old rain blooming among the stones
the constant desire for other things
whatever they are

the rain that now withers
and grows sallow
as the echo of a reed flute

and this nostalgia
that barely grazes the flesh
but mortifies the soul

can you still hear me?

consciousness like a medusa
sears this body   these words

poor exposed slumberous thing
that will end up covered by grass

or am I the one I've lost?

supplicant without restraint
hostess with empty hands

in the barren frost of her mothering

light falls
insidious
horsefly

I'm not given to know anything

so many years to make it to this morning
one like any other

to make it to this day
one like all the rest

and to receive it
as an offering

where in me are you crying?

sleep ineluctable and warm
like an open lap

like a memory of one's mother

I'm still inside the light
but it's you who must tell me
you the empty word   keeper of the name

spilled light
in the confluence of dreams
flooding the heart

absolved light
in the breadth of the instant

light alone   nothing but
unfettered
slight at its root

shattered light   harsh
arrested in its cry
trembling in its hands

and I spoke your name
and the place was made of air

and the word
prey

in the desolation of faith

and the word   a doe
collapses
in the fullness of silence
meek in its infinite contradiction
in its mercy

and the heart shuts
and the heart opens
astonishing itself

hushed light
nearly dust

are you the one who dwells in the name?
you who burst in?

Pythia bearing down
on consciousness

stammering
I wheel like a falcon in the sky

scythed light
in its astonishment

ebb and flow of the vestal years

in here the light spills over
and the word crosses the threshold

and I packed my mouth with dirt
to silence the words

water wrenching apart   if I could have touched your pale depths
wells of water   if I could have slashed open fear
water like an oyster when it's stroked
                    if I could have opened what is closed like your body
water unto dust
water kneeling in you
water enduring your thirst kneeling in you
unto dust
water begging to be kissed
clenched fist dissolving into mud   I should have told you and you wouldn't
                                          have heard me
                                      it was as if you'd never existed
                                      that you might gather me up
                                      and steal from me in my incomprehension

                        like a stone forever obedient

and I was talking to you
and you were me

      and the water was as dark

as one who surrenders her soul
and there is no one

and all that sky in your head

and the heart that refuses to sink
sinking

and I as before and as always
and always forever obeying you

I don't know how to do anything else
I've never known how to do anything else

I obey   obey you

and all that's orphaned   slit
                       open

                              and the moon pounding beneath that sky
            paler than water paler than your dreams
                                          more feeble

and you would tell me
      dream that the dream of life is beautiful
      my child

                                    do you remember?

I can't wake up

it is spring again
the plum trees are blooming

you planted them long
long ago

       and the voice would say

let me enter you
steal from you what belongs to me

do you hear my heart's disquiet?

does my longing my boundless longing
distress you?

the longing is in your mind   it says

with big blue
beautiful eyes

swollen feet
lungs full of water

disguised as an old woman
soaked to the marrow

a harpooned whale
sinking into herself

sinking into her rage
pledged with love

and the heart that refuses to sink
sinking

and I wishing to make my way to you
and the water   and darkest one

       sow me

        Rise
Mother from off me

God damn you God damn me my
misunderstanding of you

and she is so lonely
an orphan

      in the world of the dead

but this is not loneliness
it is not sadness
this flow is pure joy
though joy is always sad at its root
it is delivered like death without your knowing
it is this not knowing that flows
it enters as a body enters love

this restless beauty

Kadosh
Kadosh
Kadosh

words flood like tears

loaded words
like a fisherman's net

flayed words
like ash on the skin of a sadhu

silt words
unspoken

summer opens up
agapanthus clench the sun
blue
you let life pass by
a life spent longing
things you didn't need
you listen to yourself
decode old forgotten selves
remorse from far away
leaps like a leopard—words
meaning suddenly gone
leap
dreams soar
then fade
slow
slow homecoming
oh mother
if only I could forgive you
oh mother
if only you could forgive me

I dwell in your silence
        in this your oblivion—which is my own

the body kneels down like a sun
                and sinks

I dwell in that quiet place
      there in your hushed flow
           there in your light

now you're the one crying
        the one beseeching

                where are you crying?
            where in me do you cry?

I'm the last one
to accompany her

to help her
to die her

let her go   they say

but if I could I'd give her my pulse
if I could I'd cloak her dread in flowers

if I could I'd ask the earth itself
to absolve her

      and forgive her

forgive me
forgive me forgiven one

I kiss your fear
I kiss the loneliness of your fear

your orphaned fear
your forever more fear

your fear inside me

    and devotion like an obsidian blade
                      cuts

silence in its seed
quiet light

I'm there

the moon
more fragile than your dream

and the word

shatters capsizes
there

where it's cut

locked cell you in me
without me

and what will you say to me now?
what else will you say?

אויב דו גלייבסט אז דו קענסט שלעכטס טאן
דארפסטו טראכטן אז דו קענסט פאריכטן די אולה
אויב דו גלייבסט אז דו קענסט וויי טאן
דארפסטו טראכטן אז דו קענסט פארקיירן די וואונד

if you believe you can cause damage
believe you can mend
if you believe you can injure
believe you can also heal

ἡ μνήμη ὅπου χαὶ νὰ τὴν ἀγγίξεις πονεῖ
memory aches wherever it is touched

and maybe
        and what I am

                and it changes
            and lies at the center

the intensity of what it is

                this is how she enters the Mikveh
                this is how she immerses herself
                this is how she makes the offering
                                this is how

                        in the heart of the water

and there

      placed there
         in that old woman's
body
   I

     more mortal
than ever

  and the body

       rough
    surface
      of sprouts
      of leaves

      her skin

       mottled
    with earth

and the days there
           one
  and another

   and another

       and if this were just
a dream?

tell
   tell me

you who know me

you who are more I
                    than I am

you who understand me

                 because you I
         don't understand you

     you   yes
you

    tell me
tell me

      tell me

and the body

doesn't let
    doesn't let me

    doesn't let itself be understood

            and we can't imagine
                can't imagine

    what's happening to us

and in her loneliness
        and with me

        in his loneliness stubborn
and vain

        this I

        I love so dearly
                and who loves me so dearly

and looks at me
        and looks at herself

looking at herself
                in fascination

                with her quartz earrings
                her pearls

                her brooches from Paris

                looks at me
                        and doesn't see

                        the fat old
                                woman

                I am

                        and I do I see her?

and everyone else

what do they see
                when they see me?

and in the street
sun
　and life

　in abundance

　as if there were plenty
　as if it were

　　　forever

　　and the body trapped
　　　　　here

　　　　　and I'm there
　　　in that body

　　　　I who don't know
　　and don't want
to know

　　　that I'm
　　　　old

what shortcuts

what path

what's this
I'm feeling?

where's this
shipwreck headed

these words
these bones?

where?

what am I doing here?

my insomnia approaches
perfection

                  I'm wide awake in my dream

      it's three in the morning
               and I'm afraid

      this is what it is to be old?
                     it's like this?

and suddenly
a nostalgia
        comes over me

        perhaps the boredom
                of another me also

        forgotten

    and I cry out

            and she
        the almost
old woman

        cries out

                me?

                is
            she
                me?

the all the words are yours
I say

and the body
old sunflower
bows
under the caress

bends
shy
gently
bends

before you

the words
are yours

from you
they gather you in

from you
their flight

don't you hear them?

don't you hear me anymore?

and the voice
        tumbling

                and you
    on its edges

        on its crags and scarps

                you in this body
            that is closing

                and that asks

                is asking me for

                        what:

                I don't know

and if I end up alone
alone in the loneliness

    of this lonely body?

        who will receive it?
        who will anoint it?

        who will say Kaddish for me?

I was barely

    the one who had
        to have been

  barely
    the outline

           what should I
            have been?

did I choose my life?
    was the oracle fulfilled?

    did I obey?

        obey whom?
        for what?

which of all the lives
    that have lived me

        is most mine?
        most true?

          where is what's been lived?

          where is what I made up?
          where did I go wrong?

I would like to be consoled
for my shortcomings

for not being able to be there
when I needed to be there

that they could ask me why
                    why were you unable

                        why?

where's
    the old house?

            where's the memory?

of myself?
of the woman I was?

of you?

sunrise

the window
fills with light

        and the day
      irreversible
       in the oh so human
              morning
                  opens

   and I wake up

old sunflower
you bowed

    to no one
but Great Storm
of Equinox

from what severance comes the offering?

petals of water

       monotonous

      flapping of wings
      sundering

splinters

               and that billowing swell beneath my skin

    lightning bolt of syllables

before June
before the rains

    saudades

it rains

an initiation

as if she had drunk hemlock

she lets her do it
she watches her do it

water bursts into
the stations of her cry

near the sobbing

the quick drop

flowing

in disarray

and the body

severed branch

scent of freesias

a headlong fall

from the deepest place
I'm shattering

chalice

the dry flow

flowers a dam

the body beyond measure

and she said
    I have no more heart than the one you're slashing

                and you darker than ever
         overflow me

but I'm the one crossing the boundaries

and it drops

between me
and myself

in that January
on its slope

     plea   gash
dislocation

in this landscape

in that gorge
in that mirror

on the edges
in my loneliness

and drops

arches
sways

and the exuberant
plunge

opens this flesh

and the greedy
              body

dares not refuse

and the words

          bending
              yielding

        trembling
        yielding

   abandoning themselves

         and in that abandonment
           as they yield

           the gaze

            and that's where he kisses

           kisses that abandonment

        kisses that abandoned spot

and opened

        and seized by the gaze
            she moans

touch yourself he says
                    and I obey
and tremble

and pleasure comes in waves

capsizes

and sinks

        deeper

            and deeper

and further in

    pale

        devout

irreparable

opening

opening itself

    further

    further in

    further into itself

    furthering itself

sheer yes this self of hers

unfurling like a stain

like a raised fist

sundering like a ceiba tree

moaning

and the caresses grow swifter

and sweeter

and more unbridled

and the trembling recedes

    and the word draws near
demanding

        and suffering
in its urgency

though it has nothing more to say

I've almost stopped trembling

or did the trembling
become a plea?

out of this silence
open me like a furrow

she-wolf
flesh of dreams

could fear possibly reign

supreme?

consume my heart away sick with desire

just feel

feel

    the body feels

and she's there

    enthralled

feeling

she says she's afraid
                    says her fear
it's there in that body
                    in that fear
I let myself be touched
                    surrender to fear
                    and the fear
                              coarse
                                        brutal
                              exposed
                              there
                    at the mercy
          and like a drowned woman
like a penitent
                    kneeling
          before him
and she   she cries
                    and begs for more
                    curls up in that embrace of tears
          in that warm darkness
in her astonishing neediness

                    and the cry
              barely
        an edge
              a wing
          the light
                  on you
                      from you
              inside you
                  opening me
              in you
              for you
                  and only so
                  only so
                  purified
          from all that life
                  only so
                  could I discover you
                                in me

love has no mercy

and I who am made of words

have no words

and my heart drops

into the heart of God himself

and I tremble in your presence

in my desire for you

to be in you

as in God

راه بهشت از ریگ های جهن پوشیده است
و راه جهن پوشیده از ریگ های بهشت است

the road to heaven is paved with hells
and the road to hell is paved with heavens

and the body
     falls into itself

  falls into you

falls
    for you

           touch me there
           feel it

              do you feel it?

                   do you feel me?
                      ani ledodi vedodi li

                         ani ledodi
                         ani ledodi

is it my soul opening

to the depths

of the flesh

or am I the one opening

to this body of mine

that one day and just once

will look death

in the eye?

and it's the first morning of the first day of spring
and I leave your dream to enter mine
and the light is white
and day dawns hot
and my white bodice squeezes me
and fondling my small breasts
I push down my underpants
pull the starched sheet over me
and touch my young vulva
slip my fingers in
explore
find the pleasure spot
and linger there
my fingers ever more nimble
more precise
I close my eyes and say filthy girl
saying it excites me
and the feeling spreads
takes me completely
covers me completely
and I am this body
this rapture this vastness
I'm in the pleasure within the pleasure of pleasuring myself
and my nanny sound asleep in the hammock nearby
and the house submerging in drowsiness

and in the plaza the market starts to bustle with activity
there's orange juice and grapefruit juice
and rice milk and hibiscus tea and tamarind water
and strawberry atole and hot chocolate champurrado
and sweet tamales and Oaxacan tamales
and papayas and plums and Manila mangoes
and purple bananas and plantains
bunches of dominicos and tabascos
watermelons redder than blood
soursops like vaginas on display
bright-red capulin berries
pomegranates dribbling juice
black sapotes spilling over
mameys split open like vulvas
fat juicy pineapples
the passion fruit growing hard
and the heat entering the palm mats
entering the palm baskets
entering the sea bream
and the red buckets of shrimp
entering the lobsters
and the red rock crab legs
the bundles of freshwater crabs the mackerel for ceviche
and the clams partly opened and altogether stunned
the flaccid octopuses fainting in their ink
the oysters dreaming they're at the bottom of the sea
the tiny oysters small as pebbles from the river
the white pompanos from Michoacán
the freshwater and saltwater trout
the translucent jackfish and the sea bass
and the carp from Morelos and the scallops
and the charales their heads smashed
the large red snappers
and the shark fins

and the heat wings crashing
smashing them in the bougainvilleas
smashing the squash blossoms and goosefoot leaves
and lovage for the birds and the radishes
and clusters of loquats and ears of corn
unraveling in burlap coffee sacks
and the canary seed and amaranth
and sacks of millet and beans
and baskets brimming with chili peppers
the jalapeño morita ancho cascabel
guajillo manzano chile de árbol chilaca
and the pequin so tiny and hot and the habaneros
and mole paste green red black yellow
and poblano and sesame seeds for every kind of mole
and Oaxacan string cheese wound like balls of yarn
and ash-ripened goat cheese and farmer cheese and aged cotija
and manchego for quesadillas
and corn tlayudas and tlacoyos and mortars and metates for grinding
and braziers and palm-leaf fans
and shawls from Santa María hanging in the stone arcades
guayaberas and blouses made of linen from the maguey tree
openwork embroidery from the nuns in Aguascalientes
magical drawings from the Mayan weaver women
T-shirts that say Viva México with the eagle perched on the cactus
feverish and delirious alebrijes
and sandals soled with rope or tire tread and combs made of wood and plastic
and necklaces made of crystal and tourmaline and amber and tiger's eye
and butterflies and angels and agate and onyx and ebony
and periwinkles and ornamental combs of mother-of-pearl and tortoiseshell
and Nivea hand cream and Tío Nacho's shampoo
cross-stitched embroidered hearts
and soaps made of almonds and rose petals and oatmeal
and coconut and chamomile
and sulfur for getting rid of acne

and the overheated heat blazing with Celsius
plunging into the sweet pastries the conchas and cuernos
and the cookies with clotted cream slathered with honey and María cookies
and myrtle candies and quince and guava jellies
sweet potatoes from Puebla and pine nuts and chickpeas and pumpkin seeds
and rolling tobacco and vanilla from Papantla and cinnamon sticks
and swallows swinging on strands of light
and filaments of heat dangling
and roots dangling from God knows where to God knows where
and arnica and rue and aloe leaves
and ether capsules and bunches of eucalyptus leaves
and basil and myrtle and white lágrimas
and glorias for the altars
and votive candles and altar candles and cards printed with images of saints
and miraculous medallions and scapulars
and amulets to ward off the evil eye
and sticks of incense and crystallized copal
and a riot of voices
and birds full of cages
and cages of parakeets with clipped wings
and foulmouthed green parrots cursing blue streaks
and the church bells calling the faithful to mass
and music here and music over there
and flocks of lorikeets
and mockingbirds from other landscapes and other memories
and the sharp trill of yellow canaries
and the organ grinder cranking the handle round and round
and cranking out the same old hurdy-gurdy tune
and a violin sad and lean
and a daydreaming guitar
and an out-of-tune trio singing:

> tú me acostumbraste a todas esas cosas
> y tú me enseñaste que son maravillosas...

and music and more music
and noise and more noise within the noise
and from the Isthmus come the Tehuanas and the Juchitecas
and the women from Salina Cruz braids twined like snakes
great-breasted women with nipples of poppies
magnificent medusas with iguanas on their heads
medusas with gold filigreed earrings and embroidered huipiles
used to holding the reins
used to gluttonous feasts
used to drinking binges
used to pleasuring themselves rubbing their clitoris with coconut oil
used to suckling men as well as children
used to sucking penises like hard candy
used to excessive heat
letting themselves be deflowered by men's fingers
letting themselves be covered in the petals of blood from their deflowering
letting themselves be kissed in their blood
wearing ragged petticoats made of lace
and the market filling with clamorous Zapotec vowels
and the voices filling with flowers
and a lover knocking back one beer after another to get up his nerve
and a marimba its heart in splinters
drinking themselves drunk and accompanying themselves they sing:

> *ay, Zandunga!*
> *qué Zandunga, mamá por Dios!*
> *Zandunga que por ti lloro*
> *prenda de mi corazón!*

and the heat melting into the slabs of chocolate
and the guero chilies sweating and the serranos
and the poblanos for stuffing wilting
and the chard and purslane and mushrooms wilting
and the corn smut and maguey worms
and chapulines and ant larvae wilting
and the avocados and jicamas and cilantro and parsley
and peppermint and romaine lettuce and amaranth greens
and pápalo and tomatillo and epazote wilting
and onions rummaging for their hearts
and tears turning red with the heat
and the red wilting inside the red
and women selling pinole and cocoa powder
dozing where they sit
and their ragamuffins dangling from their dangling breasts
and enameled bedpans and washbasins
and earthenware pitchers for keeping water cool
and women from Campeche selling sandals
and belts of snake and lizard skin
silver needles for embroidering
and ox horns carved with mermaids and crucifixes
and the barber shop in the shade of a ziricote tree
and a mirror shard tied to the trunk of the ziricote
and the customers gazing at themselves
and the gaze gazing at itself with pleasure
and beauty real or imagined gazing at itself in delight
and all around people helping with bags of groceries
and old people getting up early should death arrive
and the people who get high on toloache
and those who get high on flower nectar
and the vendors of beeswax to keep from hearing time
those who peel prickly pears without feeling the thorns
the thorns inside the dreams
make-believe angels with make-believe wings

pulque castaways foundering in dizziness
and those who sip mezcal day in and day out
and don't know if it's Saturday or if the week's just starting
crackpots flying high as kites
lovers in a state of grace
those illuminated by the Holy Spirit
those who can see what ails you by looking at your iris
those who can see your future by studying your palm
the seers of the tarot and those who see without seeing
and those who do spiritual cleanses and who cast spells
and Chinese men who cure you with needles
and the Babalawo invoking fate with the oracle of Ifá
and Our Lady of Charity cloaked in compassion
and Our Lady of Guadalupe cloaked in roses
those who paint their dreams on amate paper
those who decipher the hieroglyphs of dreams
heat eroding in dreams
and the dreams shattering as if made of glass
the cries of children playing marbles
the cries of children playing soccer
the hard-core gamblers playing with their lives
death which is nothing but the other side of the deck
and cockfights spurs slashing to the death
place your bets gentlemen slap those greenbacks down
let the money flow let the blood flow let the tequila flow
don't chicken out on me now don't get cold feet on me now
don't duck and run on me now lay your cold cash down
there's no place for fear here
remember no pain no gain
remember life is just a game
remember if not now when
remember we're all here on borrowed time
step right up gentlemen step right up
because we're all going to die

and the heat its snout agape
and its gluttony and panting
and the morning stretching out defenseless
and on the other side rain
behind the hills
behind the mountains
great sheaves of green rain
crumbling like the skin of sinkholes
drowning in this heat
lightning bolts of doves
and the sun with its even whiter striations
tumbling down with its mantle of wasps
and bumblebees and flies
unperturbed magnificent dazzling
circled by black grackles
and the people fanning themselves
and the sweat trickling down
and the clothes getting drenched
and my panties are wet
and my sex sticky
and in the dirty market bathroom
I touch myself and come and pee on myself
and the boundless frenetic heat
and Our Blessed Lady of Guadalupe
and her offerings wilting
and the cuetlaxóchitl flowers getting scalded
and the spikenards losing their erections
and the heat dropping its petals
and the nectar spilling over
and the flowers hot and horny
and the drunken petals
clinging to the stem clinging
until they can't hang on any longer
and die

and outside the market birds of paradise
and lilies and daisies and wallflowers
and orchids naked as animals
and roots like bunches of green veins
and hyacinths and chrysanthemums and lilacs and water lilies
and heliotropes and anthuriums and jasmine flowers
and hydrangeas with washed-out colors
and azaleas with broken branches
gardenias drowning in their petals
and foundering in the perfumed silk
of a geisha's kimono
inconsolable gusts of sunflowers
bouquets of cempazúchitl for the departed
and the flowers drooping
and the living passing the bottle of aguardiente
and music and music and more music
and the sorrowful sorrow of the dead growing deafening
and the most sorrowful of all so trampled and so deaf
and so died and so dead
that she no longer even knows how deadified she is
and the flowers weeping
and the living living
and guzzling their lives
guzzling it in big gulps
and guzzling their fear
and life is such commotion
and so many days peeled away
and heat like a tormented soul
and desire biting the heart
and poisoning it like a scorpion's sting
and orange blossoms for the brides who've already tasted love
and orange blossoms for the spinsters and the girls receiving First Communion
and for the women who have married God
and preserved their hymen intact

and bouquets of tiny white clouds
and ecstatic daffodils
and bouquets of Queen Anne's lace and forget-me-nots
and D. H. Lawrence's pansies
opening in all their beauty
and begonias and geraniums irises freesias
and pelargoniums and petunias and violets and tulips
and dahlias and nopalillos hot bothered and surly
and cactuses shriveling in their clay pots
and thorny crowns of Christ dripping coral blood
and the blood blooming with thorns
and peacock wings gazing at one another eyes wide open
and bales of hay and alfalfa for cattle
and bales of rushes and ostrich feathers and calendulas
and clusters of stars and bundles of heliconia
and bundles of red carnations and roses plenty of roses
and there's the girl Diego Rivera painted
with the calla lilies
and the photograph of my Russian grandmother in Xochimilco
on a punt piled high with calla lilies
now forgotten in a cigar box
and I see my grandmother from Puebla in her mansion in Las Lomas
and the dog days of summer are overflowing
and petals stain the air
and the veranda so white it vanishes from my sight
and I vanish into the memories
and I see my mother placing calla lilies
in a Talavera pitcher and on the radio
they're playing the boleros she likes so much
and I see my nanny and I see that girl who is me
bringing my mother calla lilies
and I see myself today now here
here after all these years
and in a vase I have some calla lilies

and I'm listening to the same boleros my mother listened to
and time dissolves into multiple times
and my life is made up of multiple lives
my nanny and I eat in a diner
we order tasajo and bone-marrow soup
I gulp down a frosty Coca-Cola
and it's so delicious it brings tears to my eyes
my nanny buys me cotton candy
buys me anise-flavored mints
and I'm throwing a tantrum
she buys me a lemon ice
and the tantrum passes
my nanny Lupe doesn't say much
she's from Oaxaca and doesn't know much Spanish
she takes me to mass unbeknownst to my parents
she teaches me to make the sign of the cross
and she commends me to the Virgin of Guadalupe
oh! beloved Virgin Mother of God
comforter of the afflicted
health of the sick
refuge of sinners
mystical rose
deliver me from all evil
what can I say to you beloved virgin what more can I say to you
what words can I use when I don't know the Ave Maria
what words can I use when I'm so afraid
you would have to open the wound
the deep the true wound
open it there in that breach
and in all those many and wounded days
and in all those many lapses
and in that plunder and in the violence I wreak on myself
and in all those many years in which I wasted myself
and forgot myself

and I accuse myself because I did that and more
and all that and more so my mother would love me
and all that and more to deserve her love
and I continue to love her and continue to obey her
and even in her death I continue to obey her
and even against my will I continue to obey her
and it is for her that I offer my damage
hallowed be thy name
pray for us
pray for us
pray for us
I don't even know how to pray to you beloved Virgin
I don't know the Our Father nor your litanies
Mother conceived without sin
it is I who have sinned
I who have been unable to become myself
and the orphaned soul there
there at its root
and my nanny tells me about her nahual
and tells me that little white girls don't have animal spirits
and that I will be forever alone and defenseless
and I hug her tightly and cry with her
and she wraps me in her shawl
and the shawl smells of dampness and sweat
never ever again did I smell that smell
hers and hers alone
one day she ran off with the gardener
she must have died long ago
for me she died the day she left me and took off
she is by my side in nearly every photo of me as a girl

where's what I've lived what I thought I'd lived?
where's the dream I once was the one I continue being?
where all those people and all those days that disappeared
like in those cemeteries with no names
no dates just shards of shattered pottery

I'm here in what's most fully forgiven
there's no guilt
there's no repentance
there's nothing to forgive
there's fear

I'm in Polanco Park the old Polanco Park
with the same Clock Tower the same benches
the same pond and the same old Iztaccíhuatl
the volcanic Iztaccíhuatl fierce and alone and in the loneliest part of love
goes on dreaming

and one speaks of what one sees
and one speaks of what one does
and one speaks of this and that
and what is most true is kept silent
what is most true is not spoken

and the plum trees awash in flowers
and that girl on the bicycle that's me
and I let go of the bike's handlebars
and let go of them so you will watch me
                              look at me
look how I don't fall
look how strong I am
look at my hands embracing the wind
look what I can do
                    you're watching aren't you?
look at me here I am
here with you
            you see me don't you?
            you hear me don't you?

come so I can tell you everything I wanted to tell you
and never did
come
        don't you feel how much I love you?
        don't you feel my love?

and the wound there to be wounded
and one grows accustomed to the injury
and the wound grows deeper
and the pain more unbearable
and you're taught to stand it
and one day you and the pain both fester
and you can't contain the pain any longer
and there's no one to defend you from yourself
there's no longer anything nor anyone
anyone nor anything only you
only that you that is you

and I'm in that broken orphaned place
faithful as a dog

to what lengths can I go against myself?
to what lengths will I go?
to what lengths?

Lady of the Unfathomable
Merciful One
whether you exist or not
I need to believe in you
I need you come
come and enter that salt marsh
that ocean surge that lament
its reefs its sharp edges
enter and cover them
cover their affliction and remorse
cover them as you cover those who drowned for love
and those who drowned for lack of love
gather them up come
gather me up too come
come and ease this fever
ease this anger
come to my side come
come and soothe me come
come and kiss the wound

kiss it that something like a glint of light
might filter into this so deserted place
bottomless incomprehensible
hermetic
parched
sealed
out of reach

who is praying? is it me?
who is answering?
where do these words come from?

and who who will say Kaddish for me?

and fear there
frozen there
indestructible there
clenched there
immovable stillness
unending stillness
and fear lunges
and detaches my retina
I can't see can't see can't see can't see
can't see where I'm hurting myself
can't see the wound can't see
and there I am
there at the peak
I can't see the damage
can't see the plundering
can't see can't see

I have to open my eyes
I have to open them
I have to see the damage
I have to see it
I have to see
I have to see
          and can't see
I can't see can't see
can't see

and the fear overflows
and keeps me from thinking
and keeps me from understanding
and keeps me from doing anything
and I can't do anything
and I don't want to do anything
and I don't want to see anything
and I can't see anything
I'm inside the fear
there where it hurts the most there
there I am

and the fear turns to pleading
and the anger turns to pleading
and the pain to pleading
and even fear itself is nothing but pleading
and the words plead
and I plead
it's obedience in another form
and I've been taught to obey
and I'm obeying
and letting that fear pound me
and I have no means to defend myself
I'm helpless against it
and then I ask for forgiveness I don't know what for
I don't know why
and I beg I beg you don't leave me
don't leave me don't leave me don't leave me
and one doesn't beg for that
and I'm begging for it
begging like a beggar woman
I have no shame
I'm afraid
I'm so afraid

and then oh yes! then there are those the other days
the inexplicably gorgeous ones
and the dreams of love
even if they're only dreams
and boleros splintering one's heart
and the red perfume of the red carnations
and the lightheadedness this feeling brings
oh! if I could only sink into the Castalia
and be cleansed
as if I'd gone to the Mikveh for you
for you to take from me what is yours
to die of love
even when there's no love
the beginning is there
there where the beginning begins
there the overflowing
the enormous overflow there
there knowing that's how it should be
that it has always been so
that we know nothing
that it's always the first morning
always the first day
and that's all that's all
that's all we know

and the moon higher and more naked than the wind
shattering in that sky
as violently blue
as a swarm of stars

        tell me about fear what do you know about fear?

and there's the moon quicksilver
unerring as Artemis
the moon with white lioness claws
the moon hiding in the scrub
ready to lunge at my flesh
concealed there in this heat
there where I too am hiding
there where I let myself be licked between the legs
let myself be kissed there
there beneath that silent music
dazed by the heat there
exposed there I beg there I beg you there
drunk with desire there
in that sweltering heat there
in that immensity there
I touch there I guide him there
with my hands I help him there
and he lets me guide him lets himself be guided
does what I ask him to do
does it in the voluptuousness
of the moon in its radiance
does it weeping
and prostrate I weep as well
and beg for more

and the moon climbs onto the rooftops
and the heat saps her strength
and lets her fall
and strips her and splits her
and breaks her
leaving a white stain
a petal
a thread
an unspoken fear
that turns to mud
leaving the moon burnt by the sun
leaving the dried blood
leaving the moon's shadow
leaving an echo among the rocks
leaving a broken sound

and though she is the one who governs the menstrual cycles
and though she makes no concessions to menopause
and can be merciless with hot flashes
and cramps and mood swings
now the moon is nothing but a breath
a shattered dream

I've sunk into that dream
I've sunk into you

                       are you afraid too?

and the moon lingering on the edges of the bed
and slipping gentle and white between the sheets
and you and I kissing each other our eyes shut
and sunken down to the ultimate fear sunken
down to the even more sunken kisses
sipping one another
sinking into one another

look at me
look how I open myself
look how open I am for you

and your greedy nimble fingers
delve deeper penetrate
and the pleasure grows more intense
more powerful
more ruthless
obscene exquisite
overpowering
and then I pee like a little girl
and my cry is also that of a little girl
and the moon hides
and leaves us alone
and on our own
and everything else ceases to exist
all that exists is you and me

the torment of ecstasy
the fall into the other into otherness
happiness surpasses pleasure

and I my legs spread open
my arms spread open
my sex spread open
trembling
spilling over
sweaty crucified
I'm dying of love

I know that love has that power
I know that this death is exuberant
I know that to deserve it
I must let my heart be consumed
I knew it from the first kiss
I know that it took me a lifetime to know this
I know that I might never have known

and the defenseless body yields to pleasure
yields to that pleasure takes pleasure itself
oh what things we do to each other
without knowing what we're doing

there I am an offering
licking you like a bitch
licking your hands licking your feet
licking your sex
running my tongue up and down you like a bitch
my kisses invisible tattoos
small wayward roe deer
seeking their mother's scent
my kisses

my trembling kisses
trembling under that dark moon
dark like a pearl from the South Seas

what are the days to me if I lose my love for you?
what are they if I lose the beauty of my love for you?
what are they if I lose the terrible beauty of my love for you?

and beauty flaying itself
flaying itself in its loveliness

and the sweltering heat so alone
so alone and so absorbed in itself

and I don't need to eat
and I don't need to sleep
and I've no need for the days
and I don't need the nights
I live not knowing about myself
I live not living in myself
desire contains everything
lays waste to everything
I'm the servant of mad
bottomless
ungraspable passion

and what will remain
            of all of this?

and I beg for more beg for more
and more and more

and more

and his tongue thrusting into the crevice of my sex
and you letting yourself go giving yourself
and he taking you farther and farther
and you letting yourself go farther and farther
                                    and farther and farther

and for an instant the light
spills over the light
and the light is dazzled
and blinded
and that's when the Mystery is revealed
and so fleeting is its manifestation
and so short-lived its appearance
and so dark its sudden radiance
and so dark the pleasure of its radiance
and so hidden the more it's revealed
so hidden the words
cannot name it
and the stars have no mercy
and the instant is lost
and I am lost in it

and the pleasure bursts and he licks it
and love comes on me like a wild beast

what did I do with my life?
what did I do with my life?
how badly did I damage it?
how badly did I let myself get damaged?
how badly did they damage my life?

where is that orphaned place?
where does it pound in me?
where do the words pound? where
when what is pounded has no words?

and the fear there in that other fear
the one farther inside the one most feared
growing there like a cancer

the fear there
crouched down there
inescapable there
stalking me there
nothing can hold it back
it's absolute
like love of God
like love of you
like taking holy vows
and cloistering myself in myself

and forgiveness does not forgive me it needs time lots of time
time to forgive

and there's no more time

and the madness is calmer now
and more subtle and more crazed
and when I finally can cry about it
it will no longer matter

and my mother is more scared than I am
and is more orphaned than I am
and I bear her fear
and do what she wants
and I am what she wants
and the prohibitions stand
and the punishments stand
and that's where I dwell
there I take shelter
there I find serenity
there in that hollow in that lack
in that hole there

and roses bloom
roses like arteries
roses spurting blood
        mother I am wounded
        mother you wounded me
        mother you pillaged me
        mother you damaged me
        let me out of you
        let me out

and from what mother do I flee?
and what mother flees from me?
happy is he who flees from his mother
says Lezama Lima
and whom do I flee when I carry my uterus inside me
from whom if I can't leave that womb
can't leave and my mother
has grown cold and is done
and I'm hungering there hungering for her hunger
there inside the mother that was mine
there inside the mother I invented
and each of us devours the other
and our hunger is never sated
and I'm the mother too

and the photographs lay there forgotten
and this dialogue is an almost voiceless monologue
and this is where the voiceless words kneel down and break apart
and this is where the crying girl clinging to her dead mother
goes on crying inside me

and the plum trees filling with birds
and the branches taking root in the earth
and in the pantry the jars of marmalade
sealed with wax

and my mom grew old and on a Sunday
and that day she put on one blue shoe and one black shoe
and without noticing and wearing her pearls
and her jade brooch and those absurd shoes
and the desolate desolated desolation of those shoes

and she never quit smoking
she smoked to her last day
and drowned in herself
and I was left without her
and with all of her that I carry inside me

it starts to rain
the rain pounds the rocks
pounds
pounds the clouds
the pounded clouds
pile up like seals
it pounds the moon
the pounded moon drowns in the water
the pounding grows harder and harder
more precise
more desperate
and the rain is relentless
it pounds like a whip
pounds like fear
pounds without pity
implacable it pounds
it won't stop pounding
won't stop raining
it rains and rains
and rains

and the oracle shatters
the line that holds it shatters
the protective net shatters
and there I am still obeying her
and there she is drowning
and there I am drowning in her

באשערט באשערט
עס איז באשערט
es iz bashert
es iz bashert
es iz bashert
it must be so
so it was written
where is it written?
how can it be written?
does fate precede the aleph?

I cover your fear with kisses
the earth will cover you
the earth will cover all your fear
and oblivion will cover the fear

and the solstice bows before the mother
                              and feeds her
and she feeds this dream
and I am in that dream

and the dream is suddenly interrupted
as if bitten by a snake

my answers were more complex than my questions
what I truly am escapes my understanding
I don't know who in me decides for me
and I leap from the pinnacle into the abyss
and get tangled in my own wings

and each day is unique unpredictable imperfect
only the void is perfect
and life is full of imperfections
and I don't know how to live it

and what remains?
what will remain?
what of what I once was?
what of me?

and all that I didn't do
and all that I didn't say
and all that I didn't give
all that I kept
                    what for?
    for whom did I keep it?

are you crying?
        I don't know

        perhaps it's you who are crying

and whom do I call out to like Job before God?

before whom do I question myself?

to whom am I talking?
who is talking to me?

and the voice with its ringing dactyls
and the madwoman with her even madder vowels
and its accents and umlauts
and its periods and commas
is dying
clawing tooth and nail it's dying on me
and here I am alone alone alone alone alone
and she saying to me that she has nothing more to say to me

and the mother on the wide veranda
plays mahjong with her friends
and smokes one cigarette after another
and the women are absorbed in the game
and smoke and drink coffee
and I'm older now than you
and I dye my hair like you
and wear your pearl earrings
and look like you
and you're dead
really truly dead
more dead and more alone
and more helpless than I

and I return to you as before and as always I return to you
look at me here I am here in your dream here with you
here in the brilliance of the sun

and on the table forgotten in a glass of water
are the red carnations of this dream

no one's here?

no one?

not even me?

tell me what do I do with all this fear?

what do I do?

She says:

      you must return to yourself
      you must return

She says:

> you're living the beauty of being alive in this life of yours
> here in your body here are your wings

She says:

> why do you tell yourself you no longer feel loss
> at losing your life?
>
> why do you tell yourself that lie?

let the word come to you
let it signify the name
let it be dark and quiet
the name does not name itself
it is named by its presence
by its echo its resonance
the name is not spoken
let the word flow
let it seep into the blood
let it bleed out within you
don't try to understand it
don't question it
let it be
let it born
let it beating
mute as the name of God
wash it bathe it sanctify it
she is the one leading you to her
look her in the face
she is inside you
know that she is blessed
know that she is not the fruit of your womb
know that she is in everyone and belongs to no one
know that she has blessed you

She says:

> you did not know love
> now you do
> this is the answer you were looking for

She said:

> I am the Word
> I am she who is born giving birth to herself
> open yourself that you may be filled by me
> open your sex for me open it
> and feel how I penetrate and impregnate you
> open yourself to the pleasure of being pregnant with what cannot be said
> and which you now know
> feel it
> let it flood you
> don't be afraid
> I'm here
> here in you and with you
> rejoice in me and in your life
> the only one and yours and of you and for you
> this is the only eternity you will ever have
> give birth to yourself
> push yourself out
> and name me

פאר זייו טויט, האט דער רבי סוסיא אזוי געזאגט:

"ווען דו וועסט זייו אנטקעגו די טיר פון הימל וועט מעו דיך נישט פרעגו,

'פארוואס ביסטו נישט געוועו משה רבינו?'

די פראגע איז: 'פארוואס ביסטו נישט געווען סוסיא?'"

פארוואס ביסטו נישט געווען דאס וואס נאר דו האסט געקענט זייו?

shortly before his death, Rabbi Zusya said:
"when I stand before the gates of heaven I won't be asked
'why were you not Moses?' but 'why were you not Zusya?'"
why did you not become what only you could be?

she says:
        touch

        do you feel it?

               do you
        feel it overflow you?

that flow

        that joy

look at it

        it is unspoken

it is yourself

        you
in you

        I speak of the pulsing

               it's not the light

                    it's you

           steeped in light

        your heart steeped in light

        light dissolved in chlorophyll

                    can you hear it?

it flows

leans

gentle

moist

says:

do you hear?

it's your breath

and what you would have wished to be
and more

and more

I can't explain it
    but

this is what I am
these are the days

life
    and

            where
in me
        am I?

where?

            and this joy verging
                on blue
                        like a vacant lot

            is like an eagle

                        a quetzal

                hey   don't go
        says a voice
                inside
        me

                        stay

I'm here

and let myself stay

    I hear my breath
    that is also yours

      I don't know who I'm speaking to

          the journey
    through the loneliest place

           has to be
       shared

         and the moon
    in which Li Po drowned

            drops
   into the pool

and I
   who am always other

      and myself

          here

   in this year of my life
   that is every year

here

    in the heat
of the end of summer

    here where I feel

          tall

      invincible

    like a sequoia

      like a young mare

fleet

      unpredictable

and in flight

       the word

       there

    where the light

bends

the sun
astonished

among the narcissi

what do I do
with so much
beauty?

and if I found myself
without words?

be bold

      gimme

        eat
from my hand

      overflow me

       word

in your bounteous
mercy

  will you leave me?

            and if I say
        it's the soul

  what am I saying?

where
have I been
am I now

where did my life go
the one I lived

where
the one I've yet to live

and if I'd been someone else
I'd be the same someone else

I have no other life
than this one
that lives me

and I with her
in her

in what I am

and in what else
I also
am

and know not what it is

mine my own
my life
altogether

and if I'd known
what would I know?

kneading of light

river mouth

brightness

as if her heart had
failed

as it is in God

—in what we call
God—

and there I am

like someone watching
like someone listening

I the intruder
the one you foretold

wait

and tremble

that human trembling

in your presence

and there's no air

ah you who I've
        been waiting for

  in your joy
I ask for
    that which satisfied

  satisfies

        who is that
            who makes me
        who
    I am

        and what for

        and why
    am I?

feel

　　yes you can

　　feel

　　do you feel it?

　　it drenches

penetrates

　　　aches

　there

　in its beauty

　　　it aches
in you

she says:
　　　take me

　　　　　　open me

　　open yourself in me

and joy

       bows

       deeply

aches

       its coarse beauty aches

                its silence

       aches

       and September's sky
   drops
down to me
       warm

       and covered in fog

       and I
           who one day
       will die

                am here

     in this moment
  that is every moment

I am alive

Adonai Eloheinu Adonai Echad ("the Lord is our God, the Lord
   is One"): A fragment from the Shema Yisrael, one of the most
   important of Jewish prayers.
alebrijes: Fantastic surrealist creatures made of wood and cardboard
   and painted by hand, from the Mexican state of Oaxaca.
amate: A type of paper made from tree bark and used since pre-
   Columbian times for writing, drawing, and painting.
ani ledodi vedodi li ("I am my Beloved's and my Beloved is mine"):
   These words, from the Song of Songs, are still spoken today by
   brides in traditional Jewish marriage ceremonies.
atole: A drink prepared with toasted *masa* (corn hominy flour)
   mixed with water or milk.
Babalawo: A Cuban *santero* (priest) in Santería, an Afro-Caribbean
   religion.
bashert: A Yiddish word that means "fate." *Es iz bashert*: "It must
   be so," or "It's meant to be."
Bola de Nieve: Ignacio Jacinto Villa Fernández (1911–1971), a singer,
   composer, and pianist from Cuba, and one of the great artists
   of the bolero.
bolero: The bolero is a romantic, slow, and sensual style of music,
   created in Cuba at the beginning of the twentieth century.
   Among its most acclaimed composers are Bola de Nieve, José
   Antonio Méndez, and Frank Domínguez, from Cuba, and Au-
   gustín Lara and Armando Manzanero, from Mexico.

Castalia: One of the natural springs near the oracle at Delphi, where the nymphs would bathe.

cempazúchitl: The Mexican (or Aztec) marigold, an orange flower native to Mexico, commonly used in rituals during the Day of the Dead celebrations.

champurrado: A Mexican drink, typically made of ground corn, dark chocolate, water, and vanilla.

chapulines: The Mexican Spanish word for grasshoppers, from the Nahuatl. In Mexico they are commonly eaten with garlic, salt, and ground chili peppers.

charales: A small freshwater fish found in Mexico, typically sold and cooked dried.

conchas and cuernos: Two types of Mexican pastries, whose names reflect their shapes: seashells (*conchas*) and croissant-style horns (*cuernos*).

copal: A name for tree resin, particularly the aromatic resin from the copal tree. Copal has been a key element of Mesoamerican medical traditions and religious rituals since pre-Columbian times.

cuetlaxóchitl: Poinsettia, also called Christmas flower, a flowering plant native to Mexico.

dominicos and tabascos: Two of the many types of bananas cultivated in Mexico. *Dominicos* are the shorter and sweeter of the two.

epazote: An aromatic plant used as a seasoning in a variety of Mexican stews.

guayaberas: Short- or long-sleeved men's shirts, typically made of linen or cotton and decorated with two vertical rows of embroidery and patch pockets at the breast and waist. They are commonly worn in the south of Mexico and throughout the Caribbean.

Haggadah: A Jewish text that sets forth the order of the Passover Seder and that tells the story of Jewish liberation from slavery in Egypt as described in the Book of Exodus in the Torah. The first Haggadah was compiled in the tenth century.

huipiles: Traditional, loose-fitting tunics worn by indigenous women from central Mexico to Central America. These garments are usually decorated with colorful designs, often embroidered or woven by hand.

iguanas: Large, tree-dwelling lizards native to Oaxaca, as well as other tropical regions of Mexico, Central and South America, and the Caribbean. The iguana is in danger of extinction.

Iztaccíhuatl: An inactive volcano in the Valley of Mexico, also known as "the Sleeping Woman."

Kaddish: A hymn of praises to God. In the context of the dead, it refers to the Mourner's Kaddish, part of the Jewish mourning rituals included in all prayer services, as well as at funerals.

Kadosh Kadosh Kadosh ("Holy, Holy, Holy"): From the Hebrew קידוש (*kiddush*): to sanctify or consecrate. This is part of the Amidah, a prayer in the Jewish service, as well as the beginning of the Sanctus, a hymn in the Christian liturgy.

Kol Nidre: The prayer that begins the service on Yom Kippur, also known as the Day of Atonement, the holiest day in the Jewish religious calendar.

Lethe: From the Greek Λήθη, meaning oblivion or forgetfulness. One of the rivers of the underworld whose water bestows oblivion on those who drink it.

Li Po (701–762): One of the most prominent and acclaimed poets of the golden age of Chinese poetry in the Tang dynasty, also known as Li Bai.

mameys: Fruit with a dark orange-colored flesh, native to Mexico. Split in half, the mamey resembles a vulva.

metates: From Nahuatl, the name in Spanish for rectangular mortars made of volcanic stone. They are used to grind a variety of things, including corn for making tortillas.

Mexico Park: This park, built in 1927 in the Hipódromo Condesa neighborhood, is one of the most beautiful parks in Mexico City. Beginning in the 1930s, it was a meeting place for Jewish immigrants fleeing anti-Semitic persecution in Europe.

mezcal: An alcoholic beverage made from the maguey cactus. Mezcal, also called "the drink that fell from heaven," is usually bottled with a maguey worm at the bottom. It is the quintessential drink of Oaxaca.

Mikveh: A ritual Jewish bath used for purification. The water in the Mikveh must be "living water," flowing water from a natural source, such as a spring or rainwater.

mole: The generic name for a variety of Mexican sauces, generally made with an equally wide variety of chili peppers, nuts, and spices.

nahual: A supernatural spirit in Mesoamerican folk religion. The term can refer to the person who has the ability to transform physically or spiritually into an animal form or to the animal that serves that person's alter ego or guardian spirit.

pápalo: A plant whose leaves have been used to season food in Mexican cooking since pre-Columbian times.

Polanco Park: This park, now called Parque Lincoln (Lincoln Park), is located in the heart of the Polanco neighborhood of Mexico City. It was inaugurated in the late 1930s and has been popular with families ever since, with children often sailing toy boats on its reflecting pond.

pinole: An edible powder made of ground roasted corn combined with ground cocoa beans, cinnamon, vanilla, or other spices.

prickly pear: The fruit of the nopal cactus and emblematic of Mexico. To eat it, one must first remove the skin, which is covered with spines.

pulque: A fermented, alcoholic drink made from the agave or maguey cactus, whose name comes from Nahuatl. *Pulque* is drunk primarily in rural areas and has been brewed since pre-Columbian times. It is said that *pulque* should be drunk slowly, one kiss at a time, rather than in a single shot, like tequila.

Pythia: From the Greek πυθώνισσα. Pythia was the high priestess of Apollo, the oracle at the temple of Apollo at Delphi. Possessed by Apollo, the Pythia, or sibyl, would prophesy seated on a tripod.

Rosh Hashanah: The Jewish New Year. It is the first of the Jewish High Holy Days, which culminate in Yom Kippur.

rue: A medicinal plant, used for its esoteric properties of protection.

sadhu: An ascetic monk in Hinduism and Jainism. Some sadhus walk around naked and may cover their bodies in ash.

sapotes: Tropical fruit with sweet, black flesh, whose name comes from Nahuatl.

saudades: A Portuguese word that describes feelings of nostalgia, sadness, or melancholy, or a longing for someone or something.

Shaharit: The traditional Jewish morning prayer service.

shofar: A trumpet made of a ram's horn, sounded in the synagogue during the month preceding Rosh Hashanah and at the end of Yom Kippur since antiquity.

soap plant: The amole plant, native to Mexico. Juice from the bulb of this plant is mixed with water to make soap.

Talavera: A type of glazed pottery typical of the Mexican state of Puebla since the sixteenth century. Talavera pottery is most commonly glazed in white and blue.

tasajo: Thinly sliced, salted, grilled beef, a traditional dish in the central valleys of the Mexican state of Oaxaca, often served with *tlayudas* and radishes.

tlacoyos: Oval-shaped patties made of corn *masa* and stuffed with refried beans or cheese. *Tlaycoyos* date from pre-Columbian times.

tlayudas: Large corn tortillas spread with refried beans and covered with red tomato sauce, typical of the central valleys of the state of Oaxaca.

toloache: The Nahuatl word for a type of plant with psychoactive properties, commonly used in witchcraft to cast love spells.

Torah: The Torah, the central reference of Judaism, is made up of two parts. The written part is the first five books of the Hebrew Bible or Old Testament (in Hebrew, the Pentateuch). The second part, the Oral Torah, is composed of generations of rabbinic commentary, compiled as the Talmud and the Midrash.

vanilla from Papantla: A type of vanilla from the Mexican state of Veracruz. The Totonacan inhabitants of this region call it "the black flower."

Xochimilco: A pre-Columbian canal system in the southern part of Mexico City, now a popular tourist destination. The main attractions are the brightly colored, flat-bottomed, gondola-like boats adorned with flowers, which one can rent to travel along the lake and canals.

Yiddish: The language of the Jews of central and eastern Europe before the Holocaust. Yiddish originated in the ninth century as a dialect of High German, incorporating elements of Hebrew and Aramaic. It is written phonetically, using the characters of the Hebrew alphabet. Since the Holocaust, in which the majority of Yiddish speakers were killed, this language has been vanishing.

Yizkor: From the Hebrew root רכז (*zakhor*), meaning "to remember." Yizkor is the memorial service recited four times a year in the synagogue in memory of deceased parents, children, and other relatives.

Yom Kippur: Day of Atonement, the most solemn day of the Jewish year, marked by prayer and twenty-five hours of fasting.

Zandunga: The unofficial anthem of the Isthmus of Tehuantepec.

Zapotec: A language indigenous to the people of the Isthmus of Tehuantepec and surrounding regions. There are over four hundred thousand speakers of Zapotec. The Zapotecs call themselves "the people of the clouds."

ziricote: A deciduous tree from southeastern Mexico. The wood of the ziricote is very hard and nearly black.

Zohar: Also known as the Book of Splendor, the Zohar, a core text of Jewish mysticism, was written in Spain at the end of the fourteenth century.

אבר המש שדקתיו לדגתי (*Yitgadal veyitkadash shmei rabah*): "May His great name be exalted and sanctified," the opening words of the Kaddish, a hymn of praises to God and one of the most important parts of the Jewish liturgy, which is recited in memory of the dead. It is written in Aramaic, an ancient language of the Near East.

יזכר אלהים נשמת אמי מורתי שהלכה לעולמה (*Yizkor elohim nishmat imi, morati shehalcha le'olama*): "May God remember the soul of my mother, my teacher, who has passed to eternal life..." See the Glossary entry for *Yiskor* for more information.

באשערט באשערט / עס איז באשערט ("bashert bashert / es iz bashert"): See the Glossary entry for *bashert*.

SOURCES

113 The last four lines are from "Moonset, Gloucester, December
1, 1957, 1:58 am" by Charles Olson.

124 "if you believe you can cause damage / believe you can mend /
if you believe you can injure / believe you can also heal": Transla-
tion of the Yiddish from *Licutei Moharan* by Rabbi Nachman of
Breslov.

125 "ἡ μνήμη ὅπου χαὶ νὰ τὴν γγίξειζ πονεῖ / memory aches wherever it
is touched": From "Memory I" by George Seferis.

143 "old sunflower / you bowed / to no one // but Great Storm / of
Equinox": From "Wintergreen Ridge" by Lorine Niedecker.

153 "consume my heart away sick with desire": From "Sailing to
Byzantium" by W. B. Yeats.

158 "the road to heaven is paved with hells / and the road to hell is
paved with heavens": Translation of the Farsi from a Sufi poem.

161 "the bounded is loathed by its possessor": From "There Is No
Natural Religion" by William Blake.

165 "*tú me acostumbraste a todas esas cosas / tú me enseñaste
que son maravillosas...*": From "Tú me acostumbraste," a bolero
written in 1957 by the Cuban singer-songwriter Frank Domínguez,
very popular in Mexico.

166 "*ay, Zandunga! / qué Zandunga, mamá por Dios! / Zandunga
que por ti lloro / prenda de mi corazón!*": From "La Zandunga," a
traditional song from the city of Tehuantepec, in the Mexican state

of Oaxaca. Considered the unofficial anthem of the Isthmus of Tehuantepec, its lyrics were written by Máximo Ramó Ortiz in 1853 after the death of his mother.

251 "shortly before his death, Rabbi Zusya said: / 'when I stand before the gates of heaven I won't be asked / "why were you not Moses?" but "why were you not Zusya?"' / why did you not become what only you could be?": Translation of the Yiddish from Martin Buber's *Tales of the Hasidim*.

Conversation(s) (2004, 2021)

ON MARCH 15, 2004, and on January 20, 2021, Mark Schafer and Gloria Gervitz sat down to talk about her poem and his transla- tion of it. The first time, they sat together in person; the second time—pandemic-style—was virtual. Their conversation drifts back and forth between Spanish and English and between the first and the third decade of the new millennium, punctuated by the interjections of Gloria's dogs: Ámbar and Olga in 2004, Paula in 2021. The dialogue in Spanish was translated into English by Mark Schafer and Ruby Fernández.

MS: This translation, *Migrations: Poem, 1976–2020*, is the product of an ongoing, nearly three-decades-long conversation between me and your poem and between the two of us. Likewise, this final version of your poem is the sum or outgrowth of its many previous versions. Tell me about the relationship between its different versions and editions.

GG: I began to write *Migraciones* at the beginning of September of 1976. I had a few words, a few lines that start the poem—"*en las migraciones de los claveles rojos donde revientan cantos de aves picudas / y se pudren las manzanas antes del desastre*"—and then the next two or three lines. I especially had those first two lines in my mind, but they didn't really make much sense to me.

I decided to write them down, and it was like opening a faucet. Of course, I never knew that I was entering what turned out to be a life's project. If you ask me exactly what those two lines mean, I still don't know. I honestly don't know—even now, after more than forty-four years.

Sometimes I feel that I'd like to be, say, ten years younger, with the poem the way it is now. But I know I couldn't have written the poem the way it is now if I weren't the age I am now. I needed all that life experience to be able to write *Migraciones*. I think time was a deciding factor in this last version of the poem. I also know that there are some people who prefer other versions and perhaps will always prefer other versions; they feel more comfortable when the poem was divided into different parts. But I do know, deep down, that the way I left it in this last version is the way the poem wanted to be left. In a way, I needed a whole lifetime to do this.

MS: To follow up on that, people can still access editions of *Migraciones* from earlier times in its development—copies in libraries, people sharing editions they bought long ago. How do you see the relationship between the final version of the poem and all of its previous versions over the course of forty-four years?

GG: Look, when I started making changes and adding parts to the poem, in the 1990s, I hadn't even known that some of those parts, which I'd published separately, were actually part of the poem. I honestly didn't. I thought, "Oh my goodness, what a gift! Poetry is giving me the chance to redo things—the chance life doesn't give us to redo things that we might have wanted to have done differently in our lives." But now I realize it's not true, not even with poetry. Because all the other versions also exist, so people can see the process of the poem, as well as the final version. I would have liked to have had the poem the way it is now, which is the one I prefer. But I can't deny the others, just as I cannot deny other parts of my life.

I find it striking that it has taken me forty-four years to write this book, which is the only poetry I have published, and that your process of translating *Migraciones* has been quite similar to my process of writing it. What drew you to the poem originally?

MS: I remember reading a review of the first publication of *Migraciones*, which contained a fragment from what was then called "Shajarit," in a Mexican journal in 1991. I think the aspects of the poem that had the biggest impact on me were its visual quality, the centrality of women, and in hindsight, that as Jews we shared a certain cultural identity. I think this last part resonated in me, although I didn't recognize it at the time. Three of my grandparents came to the United States from Russia and Poland in the early 1900s. I think I imagined that somehow in what you were doing there was a home for me as a reader and a translator, and maybe more.

GG: Three of my grandparents were also immigrants from Russia and Poland. They had wanted to go the United States, but it had closed its borders, and Mexico is a country that has always been generous in opening its doors to immigrants and exiles—to Jews in the 1920s through the Second World War, Spaniards in the 1930s, Argentines and Chileans in the 1970s. My grandparents were poor when they came to Mexico, and they found a warm place (both the climate and the people), a place full of possibilities. The ones who stayed in the "old country" were killed.

My maternal grandfather came to Mexico around the time of the Mexican Revolution. He was a very young man when he met my grandmother, a young Catholic lady from Puebla, and they fell in love.

I was surprised myself how this whole Jewish world burst into my writing in the first three parts of the book—themes of exile and of these immigrants and all this Jewishness that I didn't know was in me. I don't come from a religious family, but Jewishness is also an ethic, a way of being in the world.

MS: Did you study Yiddish when you were young?

GG: Yes. From third grade through high school my parents sent me to a Jewish school whose teachers came from the same part of Europe—Russia, Poland. They weren't exactly Zionists, although they weren't against Israel: they were Bundists; that is to say, socialists with a great deal of love for and pride in the whole tradition of that world that was virtually wiped out by the Nazis. I'll always be grateful to them because they taught us the great tradition of Yiddish literature, the importance of the Jews of the Diaspora, and they imbued me with pride in this heritage of Jews in exile, of that *farshvotener velt*, that lost world. But I wasn't thinking of any of this as I was writing. I remember that I suddenly began writing about this woman, whom I now see is my own invention of my paternal grandmother. I never met her, because she died a year before my parents got married. I often thought, without ever putting it into words, about what my grandmother must have felt as a young woman coming to a country she knew nothing about, and with two children and the responsibilities of running a household.

MS: What was it like for them to be Jews in a country as Catholic as Mexico? And what has it been like for you?

GG: My understanding is that my grandparents were pretty isolated, that they formed fairly closed communities. And my parents, who were neither practicing nor religious, always lived surrounded by Jewish friends. As for myself, fortunately my experience was fairly lacking in conflict. My maternal grandmother was from Puebla, and my mother was born in Mexico City. Although my grandmother converted to Judaism to marry my grandfather, the Catholicism that she grew up with remained present in her throughout her life. In my home we had a Christmas tree, and they gave me money for Chanukah, so I felt fortunate that I had both things. I went to a Jewish school, but before then I had a nanny, an indigenous woman who took me to mass. So, I grew up with both things, and in my case, it didn't present a conflict. I saw that some of my schoolmates almost felt they had to choose between being a Jew or a Mexican. But for me, it was pretty clear that I was simply Mexican and Jewish—there was no contradiction.

MS: Previous editions of *Migraciones* have included an author's dedication, an author's note, a prologue, an introduction, and dates of composition. Even before the radical transformation of *Migraciones* that took place in 2016, you had already removed all personal apparatus. The critics Raúl Dorra and Blanca Alberta Rodríguez referred to these elements of the book as "voices and feelings of the person who put herself at the service of the Poem, rather than those of the Poem itself, which demands that this sacrifice now be made."[1] To what extent did the Word take control of the Poem and you become its Pythia? And if it did so, what sacrifices did you have to make to follow this calling?

GG: I haven't sacrificed anything. But I have frequently found myself in danger, like Jonah, of sacrificing my calling. The calling isn't a sacrifice, it's a fulfillment. Nevertheless, there is nothing more difficult and perhaps nothing more scary than following that calling. Many times, I have sacrificed myself to fear, to conventionality, to silly things, to propriety. I have turned away from the calling, turned my back on it. I think of a variation on a line by Rimbaud: For the sake of decorum, I have wasted my life.

I have been surprised to discover over time that some of these things, which I had put into various editions of the poem—more personal things, where it is the author speaking and not the poem—that some reviewers gave them a weight and importance that they didn't have. It's better to let the poem speak for itself. Those things may have meant a lot to me, but they didn't mean anything to the poem.

MS: *Migraciones* has had an extraordinary if not unprecedented journey, an extraordinary evolution that resembles in many ways that of a tree or a river. I want to talk with you about the point, in 2016, when you made radical changes to the printed poem. In one interview you said, "I noticed that capital letters were fear, imposing themselves on the others."[2] And a few years later, you said, "Those section titles were dikes that blocked the flow of the poem. At that moment I also understood that the capital letters were a form of fear. Out went the capital letters and the commas that were soiling the poem. I removed everything that stood in its way."[3] Earlier editions of the poem not only contained dedications and author's notes, but the poem itself was divided into sections, each with an epigraph, and at times incorporated dedications, critical essays, photography, and more. Can you talk about this process of growth and stripping away of what was not necessary, and in particular what happened four or five years ago?

GG: Starting in 2014 and lasting perhaps until 2018 or the beginning of 2019, I had what was probably the most creative stage of my life. It was surprising, because before that I was feeling as if I were almost drowning in silence—touching it. It was like the book was getting thin, thin, thin, thin. And then suddenly it started opening, really opening again, and not at the end but around the middle. I was really living in the poem, and the poem was living inside me. I would say that time has been an incredible friend, to the poem and to me, though I would also say that it was quite frustrating. I despaired during those long, dry periods of silence, which lasted for many years. Now I see that one of the big things that helped me was time itself. Because time allowed me to have the distance I needed to be able to see the poem almost as if I hadn't written it. And that allowed me to see many, many things that were not really worthwhile or that weren't adding anything. Many of the parts that I took out of the poem—perhaps they weren't bad, but they weren't working anymore in such a big poem.

What happened was this: the Spanish publisher sent me the final galleys to review; it was ready to go to print. The poem had nine parts, with subtitles, epigraphs, etc. And then it all happened in like ten minutes: suddenly I knew, it was almost like a revelation. Seeing the poem all together, I suddenly realized that I had to remove all those sections, all the epigraphs. I suddenly realized that those capital letters were stopping the poem's flow. They suddenly looked very strict to me, almost like soldiers. And the commas just made the poem dirty. It was almost like the poem told me, "I have to flow. Take all of it out, it's stopping my flow." At that moment I saw that all these different elements were like dikes, and I just had to take them out and let the poem flow, flow freely.

Then I was very strict, and I started taking out quite a few things from the poem. A few editions later, I returned a few small parts I had taken out. In 2018, a few months after the Mexican and the Swedish editions came out, some of the lines and verses I'd taken out kept returning, like somebody who's died and comes back in your dreams to say, "I'm not gone." The lines that kept returning, that wanted to come back into the poem, I'd put them back, but not exactly where they were supposed to go. It was almost like putting a puzzle together. You think it's done, but then you see that some pieces don't fit properly. So, you take them out and put them in another place, and then you say, "Oh, *that's* where they belonged."

MS: The critic Blanca Rodríguez talks about interior migrations of the text itself.

GG: Yes, the poem has outside migrations, but mostly they're inside migrations. There were also migrations of myself into other selves, as we're always migrating within ourselves. Our priorities change with time. You're not the same person who called me thirty years ago; I'm not the same person. You're not even interviewing the person you first met thirty years ago. We've had different experiences, we've changed places in our lives, inside ourselves, outside. In that sense, the poem is always moving, just as we are.

MS: When did you move to San Diego?

GG: I moved in 2011. Why?

MS: I'm thinking of a variety of major creative works written in exile or by expatriates: by James Joyce, James Baldwin, Dante, Beethoven, exiled from hearing, or Homer, exiled from sight. In

2004 you told me, "I was surprised how the Jewish world burst into my writing." During this more recent creative period, which led to the final version of your poem, one of the things that burst into your writing was the Oaxacan market. Were you surprised at how the world of Mexico burst into your writing after you had moved from where you'd lived for your whole life until then? Do you see that as related?

GG: Yes, I do think it's related. When you're too close to something, you end up not really seeing it. You get used to it. Here in San Diego, I still miss many things of Mexico. One thing I always liked is that, ever since I was a little girl, I would go with my mother to the markets in Mexico City. I think it's when you leave something, when you migrate, you see things again: from a distance, from a different perspective. Suddenly in a way, all the markets I had been to throughout my life came back to my mind. And one of the many markets that will always stay with me was the one in Oaxaca. It's a magical market. Being far from it, I could see it really clearly.

I'm also grateful because I had a return to words again. I was starting to feel the way I had after finishing what was, in earlier versions of the poem, the part called "Pythia": as if I were touching silence, almost like touching death. I don't know. It was a very strange feeling, a little bit suffocating. It was so very necessary to have the words, and words also have that weight, because they are surrounded by silence, they're living in silence, and they are also ripped from the silence. I thought I would never again have metaphors, images, that I would never write again the way I started writing. In what previously was "Pythia," the language becomes very abstract, as if the words had become isolated. But here, suddenly, it's almost like a big, big flow again.

MS: There's the Oaxacan market and, strongly overlapping the market, the sexuality present in all the colors, shapes, and senses that burst forth in your description of it. And in that is another eruption of life into the poem: that of the heterosexual sexuality and eroticism that erupts in the poem forty years after you first began writing it. Did this surprise you—and that it happened at this stage of your life?

GG: I think that sometimes, especially if you were raised very prudishly, which I was, that you need a lot of time to become more yourself, to allow yourself to feel more, in every sense. I think in a way that happened to me. That's why I became, at this stage of life, very much myself. When I say "myself," look, I'm going to put it like this: I remember once reading something that Carl Jung said that we live half of our lives, sometimes even more than half of our lives, obeying and doing the things that are expected of us. And then, he says, if we are lucky the other part of our lives—and sometimes it's not even half of it but a little less than half—if we are lucky, after half your life has already been lived, you start being more yourself. More what you really are.

It's also a big mistake to think that older people don't feel as much, let's say, love or eroticism as young people do. I would even say that perhaps you can love with more passion, be more open to passion, to sex, to eroticism, when you're not young at all. Which also makes you more vulnerable, in many ways. I mean my body was in better shape thirty years ago than it is now. So, you're more vulnerable in every sense. Passion in older people can be just as strong, and it can move your world, sometimes even more so than when you're young. Because when you're young sometimes it's the hormones that are really doing a lot of the work. Not only do they start working again when you're older, but you're putting much more into it than when you were in your twenties or thirties. I think that's what happened: I think I was liberated in many ways with age.

MS: That leads me to another question about the autoeroticism and sex in your poem. To quote from early on in *Migraciones*: "*bajo el grifo de la bañera abro las piernas / el chorro del agua cae / el agua me penetra / se abren las palabras del Zohar*" (I spread my legs beneath the bathtub faucet / gushing water falls / the water enters me / the words of the Zohar spread open). Touching oneself, bridging the gap of our exile (from ourselves)—emotional, spiritual, physical, historical exile—that touching is an act of opening. Here in your poem, it is simultaneously an opening of the body and of the book. When the book opens the Word is revealed, but it was already there inside, there to be uncovered, discovered. I'd like you to talk a bit about sex, about masturbation, language, and discovery.

GG: I think that it's less scary to touch yourself, to discover yourself, than to touch the Other. People discover many things touching themselves. When a man masturbates it's more visible, more out in the open. But for a woman, masturbating is a combination of looking at yourself and practically sticking your fingers inside yourself. It's like entering and knowing yourself, seeing how you're put together or finding out what's going on in you or what you're feeling. I think that sometimes, in the physical act of love, the one who penetrates is penetrated. But for that to happen, you have to have a great deal of trust—because to really lose yourself in the Other is terrifying, whereas to get lost in yourself isn't so scary.

I think that something similar happens with words: they discover you as you discover them. It's like a dialogue between two who are in fact one. A dialogue that is really with the Other implies other, scary things. This autoeroticism, this dialogue with words is actually a monologue, even though those words can take you to places in yourself you never imagined. In the book, the dialogue isn't so much with the Other but with that other that is also you.

MS: The US translator and poet David Hinton talks about the Taoist idea—which he notes is older than Taoism itself—of a cycle of "pregnant nothingness" from which being emerges and to which it returns; it's a constant flow. I want to read you this passage from Hinton's introduction to his translation into English of the Tao Te Ching:

[The] origins of this oral tradition [which predates Lao Tzu's poetry] must go back to the culture's most primal roots, to a level early enough that a distinctively Chinese culture had yet to emerge, for the philosophy of Tao embodies a cosmology rooted in that most primal and wondrous presence: earth's mysterious generative force.... In the Paleolithic, the human experience of the mystery of this generative force gave rise to such early forms of human art as vulvas etched into stone and female figures emphasizing the sense of fecundity. This art was no doubt associated with the development of humankind's earliest spiritual practices: the various forms of obeisance to a Great Mother who continuously gives birth to all creation, and who, like the natural process which she represents, also takes life and regenerates it in an unending cycle of life, death, and rebirth.[4]

I see your work as part of this tradition that goes all the way back into prehistory, into that...

GG: Well, look. I'll tell you this. When I was born and they told my father that he had a little girl, he was very disappointed—he wanted a boy. He went home and thought to himself, "A daughter! What am I going to do with a daughter?" So, I always felt that my mother loved me more, and I loved her also very deeply. I was holding her hand when she died; I was with her to the very end. (She died in May of 1999.) But to my surprise—this is really one of those things that you don't know about yourself—I feel better without her, liberated in a way. This doesn't mean that I loved her less than I thought; it's just the way it is. She's probably the woman sitting at the center of my poem. I don't mean that that woman is literally my mother, but that she sits at the center of the poem the way my mother sat at the center of my life.

The dialogue, which is an inner dialogue, is with the archetypal mother you're talking about, because she's really at the center of everything. She's the one who gives life, and she's the one who takes it away. Why the woman at the center? Because in many ways, I wasn't considered worthwhile in my family, because I was a woman. To have this female principle as the protagonist of the book, to put it at the center, was for me an act of self-affirmation, a way of claiming my freedom. Of course, I didn't start writing with this idea. If I had, I wouldn't have written a thing.

In Mexico City in the 1950s and early '60s, in my environment, a woman's most important roles in life were to be a wife, to marry a nice Jewish man, and to be a good mother. I was never encouraged to get a degree or a job, to study—things like that were not to be taken seriously. Of course, that took its toll. But at the same time, since I was not very important, I was allowed to do many, many things that were not permitted to males in that society. I used to spend my afternoons reading and reading, and I'm not just talking about when I was quite young. And sometimes they would say, "What does Gloria do? Well, she reads, she writes poems. Nobody understands her poems, but that's what she does. She's a woman." That's how it worked: the forces in that world didn't give you a place, and at the same time, since you weren't given a place, you could choose your own. The world of words meant freedom for me.

MS: How did you become a poet?

GG: You don't become a poet. Either you have the gift or you don't, and then it depends on yourself, on external and internal circumstances. As a girl, I loved to read. I was writing stories when I was nine years old. If the teacher was late, they'd stick me in front of the class and let me tell the kids stories that I would make up on the spot.

The first book of poetry that fell into my hands, when I was about twenty-five or twenty-six, was *Libertad bajo palabra* (Freedom on Parole) by Octavio Paz. It was a revelation. I barely understood it, but I was stunned. It was one of the most important encounters of my life. It was like an earthquake in the core of my being. So, in early 1971, I brought my poems—which I thought were fine—to the poetry workshop at UNAM, the national university in Mexico City. There were eight or ten very well-read young men in the workshop, and I read them my compositions— they weren't even poems yet—and they destroyed every one of them. They were implacable. But that's when a whole world of poetry opened to me, and I first began reading T. S. Eliot, Seferis, Neruda, Vallejo, João Guimarães Rosa, and many others.

MS: It seems to me that you write against language—that is, language as something singular, pure, static. Your poetry contains Spanish, Hebrew, Aramaic, Yiddish, English,[5] Farsi, and Portuguese, and all without italics, as a single flow of language.

GG: Look, it's simply that words have a life of their own; they come as they choose. So, it seemed to me that to put them in italics would have been to give them a weight they didn't have, to emphasize them rather than allowing them to flow. When everything is flowing, just let it be. People said to me, "Why do you put the words in Hebrew?" For example, when I put the beginning of the Kaddish in the poem, why do I put it there like that, without italics? Or when the voice begins to speak in English, why don't I put it in another font? Because that's the way it's flowing. In reality "purity" doesn't exist. We live in a thoroughly intertextual world filled with many languages. Look, basically I write in Spanish. The poem is in Spanish, and the music of the poem is the music of Spanish, and so on. But when I've needed to use words in another language, I have. Period. The passage *"las mujeres se sientan en el suelo / yo digo Kadish por ti y por mí"* (the women sit on the floor / I say Kaddish for you and for me), for instance. If you're a Jew and you're in mourning you sit on the floor; you're practically sitting in the ashes, because you're in mourning. I wasn't going to write, "I pray for you and for me"—it's Kaddish, and that's that. It wasn't until the first edition of *Migraciones* in 1991 that I included a glossary with the poem. For readers who don't know, there's the glossary. If you don't need it, you don't use it. It's there as a service to the reader, as I am in service to poetry, and poetry doesn't need me to put all those things in italics.

MS: In my translator's note to the 2004 bilingual edition of *Migraciones*, I had to explain to English-speaking readers one thing a Spanish-speaking reader would notice immediately: that, with one, single exception, every subject in the poem— *I, you, we, they, it*—was grammatically feminine, female. Earlier, you said that masturbation for a woman is like entering and knowing yourself, like a dialogue between two who are in fact one, and that a dialogue that is really with the Other can be very scary. My question is this: Does the presence of men and masculine energy in this final version of the poem mean that the poem has entered a new phase, that the dialogue is now more with the Other? Or does it represent an embracing or facing of fear? Or none of the above?

GG: No. I think it has more to do what I was saying earlier: that you dare to get out of yourself, to be even more yourself—but because of the Other. It's the Other that makes you go more into yourself, even more than masturbation. You do that because you're very afraid. But once you lose that fear, even if just for a while, it's an opening, an opening in all senses. I think it could happen with something as strong as becoming a mother or a father or really falling in love and opening yourself to that love. Which can be a child, a lover, whatever. It allows you to let go of the fear you have of that. Because if you're going to love, you could get hurt. I bet you were very scared to be a father, because you didn't know how to be one. And you thought, "Maybe I won't do it right, maybe I won't have the strength." We invent many fears for ourselves. We enclose ourselves in fear because we believe fear protects us—and in some things it does. But when you dare open yourself, when you dare leave that fear, then almost magical things happen. And then perhaps you go back to the fear. Because what also happens in the poem, especially in the new part of the poem, is that even though fear has been in the poem from the very beginning—just as you say how the sexuality or eroticism has been there from the very beginning—it was more subdued. But suddenly, especially in the newest parts of the poem, I think fear becomes so strong, so real, it's almost a presence, a physical presence in the poem. Just as you noticed how eroticism with the Other, with this masculine part, has grown stronger, so too has fear, which has almost become like a protagonist in the poem.

Perhaps poetry is also what David Hinton said: making contact with this emptiness, this abyss that is at once a pregnant emptiness and the depths of the heights. Because for a few minutes—you can't stay there too long, it's too intense—poetry gives you wings!

MS: What do you think about a man translating your poem—this poem of women's voices?

GG: Rather than answering, I want to ask you that same question. You've told me that you were fascinated by the poem the first time you saw it. Basically, there was all this Jewishness and exile and migrations, and you had that in you, in your family. All of this is present in what were in earlier versions the first three parts of the poem, which is where you first entered it—where you dove in, so to speak. Beginning with "Pythia," in 1995, these themes disappeared. Yet the poem continued to pull at you, and you saw it through to its end, translating and incorporating four more parts in 2004, then all the rest, many years later. It's as if you grew with the poem, and the poem continued growing inside you—as well as on its own! I am tempted to ask you what part of *Migraciones* you like most. Perhaps you still like the earliest parts best...

MS: I think this is where I can't respond accurately about my own work. If I remember correctly, the fragment that first caught my eye was the scene of a woman sitting in a chair, and the poem is looking at her; she's at the center of the scene. I think there was something about a poem by a woman in which a woman is at the center of the poem that I wanted to know about and wanted to read.

GG: And why was it so important for you that it was a woman? That what first caught your attention and what kept you there was this woman in the center of the poem that another woman, the poet, is focusing on, giving voice to, and moving from one place and time to another? Did it catch your attention differently than if it had been a man?

MS: Yeah. That was one of the things that attracted me, that grabbed me. I think I could probably answer on many levels, from my own personal history to the level of culture to a Western way of looking at that picture. Because I'm male and because men have been dominant both in my personal life and in the world in which I grew up, the cost of this dominance has been the giving up of a certain knowledge. And I recognize that this knowledge is something I want and need. I don't think that it's not in me, but that for men, the loss of access to that knowledge has been the price of dominance, of holding normative status. I want to listen to the people who know things that I don't or have forgotten, so that I can learn or remember. In the case of your poem, it was crucial to me that you were a woman putting a woman at the center. That was something I immediately wanted to listen to and continued to want to listen to—although at times I *haven't* wanted to listen!

GG: Which is also a way of listening. Because sometimes when something matters to you, it can disturb you, make you confront things you haven't faced before. It's as if you need that connection in order to be able to go beyond the noes, the prohibitions. Once you acknowledge your connection with whatever it is that matters to you, then you can make the crossing.

MS: I want to ask you about something else. In an article Nicolás López Pérez wrote in 2020 about your poem, he quotes Edmond Jabès as saying that for the writer, discovering the works he or she is going to write is simultaneously a miracle and a wound—the miracle of the wound. Pain, a wise man once said, is the vastest of books, for it contains all books.[6] I'm thinking of Yizkor, the prayer that is recited in memory of parents and other family members that have passed and which was the title of the second part of the poem for many years. Other sections of the poem were titled "Leteo" (the classical Greek river of oblivion and death), "Treno" (Lament), and "Blues." And then there's the Kaddish, which has an important and recurring presence in *Migraciones*. It's the prayer

Jews recite when someone dies, and yet—it's a song of praise. I'm wondering, do you see *Migraciones* as a prayer, a howl, a cry of existential terror, a lament, a song of praise, or all of the above?

GG: I think it's not exactly for me to say. But I would dare say that it has a little bit of all of them. Again, sometimes it is one that has more presence, but then it gets diluted and there's a different one. But the Kaddish is very important. Maybe the whole book has to do with this. My brother, who was five years younger than I, died of a massive heart attack at the age of thirty-six. My mother said to me at the time that she was looking everywhere for something that spoke to her about the sorrow of losing a son. "I cannot understand the Kaddish," she said to me. "The Kaddish doesn't console me." I remember telling her that the Kaddish is a song of praise to God and also a song of thanks. It gives thanks because there once was life, which is better than if there never had been life in the first place, even though you feel the pain of having lost a person you loved. Poetry—I don't mean my own, but poetry in general— always contains something of the Kaddish: although it can speak of the saddest things, it really is a song of praise to the Word. And the Word, the possibility of the Word, is what makes us human.

I will tell you that in February 2020 I went for the first time in my life to Poland. I went to Warsaw and to Kraków because I had readings hosted by the publisher in collaboration with the Cervantes Institute in those two cities. And it was a very strange feeling going back to those places, especially Warsaw, because we were very near to the Warsaw ghetto. Part of my family came from what now is Ukraine; at that time it was Russia. But my maternal grandfather came from Poland. Once I was there, I did look like many people there, if you know what I mean—I could see my roots, okay? But it was a strange feeling altogether to be there, in Poland. I wrote a little something, sort of a way of saying thank you. Of course, it's similar to *Migraciones*, but it's almost a little poem in itself. I'm going to read it to you, because I think it answers, especially at the very end, a bit of what you're asking:

where do I return in coming here?

where do these roots ache?

I left here, departed long before I was born,

and return here born,
return here trembling,

here to see with my own eyes what my parents saw,
my grandparents, great-grandparents, generations lost in time,

return to that which was forgotten,
return to remember all that forgetting,
return to say Kaddish for all those who stayed here,

return to say Kaddish for myself[7]

So, there's a lot of the Kaddish in *Migraciones*. It's a Kaddish that I say for many people. But it's a Kaddish maybe for myself too. At least three times I say, "Who will say Kaddish for me? Who will say Kaddish for me?"

I want to add something that is almost a question for you and a question for myself. I have sometimes wondered if the poem has a heart, if there's a heart in the poem—and if there is one, where is it? Or if it doesn't have a heart and it's a little bit like onions: you peel and peel and peel them, but they don't really have a heart. I would sometimes ask myself that question, when I had the poem in sections, and I almost did feel that perhaps the heart was… whatever. Now I don't know, and I don't even know if it's important. But I still ask myself: "Does this poem have a heart?"

MS: At the point when you sent me the transformed version of the poem, probably in 2017, I remember it felt like returning to a childhood home: I went in, and the rooms were laid out differently. The entranceway was where it was before, but then there was a hallway that hadn't been there before, or one room connected to another room that didn't exist before. The envelope of the house was the same, but inside were all these things that were familiar and all these things that were strange. At that point I really struggled, I think for about a year, as to whether I wanted to and felt able to continue on this journey with you and with the poem. The poem seemed at this point too complex for me to fully grasp as a whole, which I felt I had before. I know that wasn't true, but I had that illusion, or familiarity. Eventually, I decided that I was on this journey: with the poem and with you.

So, one of my answers to your question is that I don't feel at all able to talk about the poem as a whole, as a single body that would have a heart. I think I just can't see it, if it's true; I'm too immersed in the poem. My other thought is *migraciones*—migrations—and that difference between migration and exile, though they can overlap a lot. Exile is when for some reason you can't go back: going back is untenable or too dangerous or you've been banished. But migration is different: Animals that migrate, they migrate from one home to another. The migration itself is movement, growth, life, which is motion. Maybe heart isn't the right word, but I guess the heart is what keeps the flow, the beat going, what keeps life going. The flow or beat of your poem has been so powerful for so many years. Perhaps heart isn't the right concept; rather, there's a life force driving the poem. Maybe it's movement itself.

GG: I like your answer, it is a good one. Maybe the movement of the poem is its heart.

MS: This makes me think of Rose Minc, who wrote about your poem early on, in the late 1980s, before the poem was even called *Migraciones*. I think she understood something essential about your poem when she noted how a feminine discourse based on metonyms—nonhierarchical conjunctions like *and*—is its essential grammar. In an article from 1987, she observed that this textual strategy, which occurs throughout your poem, also occurs notably in the Old Testament, particularly in Genesis, one of the prototypes for telling a creation.[8] In contrast, she noted that male discourse tends to be hierarchical and structured, relying on sequential or hierarchical language. Already in the 1980s, Minc saw metonymy as central to your poem. I wonder if this idea of a heart, the idea of a center, is not what's important about or relevant to your poem. It's the flow you've talked about—the life, growth, and sloughing off of the parts that become unnecessary—that's the active principle of the poem. It's different from a heart.

GG: I think you just said something very interesting. When I was writing the poem in sections, the sections were connected, but they were defined and separate, which made it easier: one section, then another, then another. And each one had its subtitle, its epigraph. I remember telling you long ago that one of the more prominent or visible elements in the poem is water, which is a feminine archetype. Like I was saying, the revelation I had in 2017, when suddenly I knew that all that structure had to go, and it's as if I gave myself permission to cut it and just let the poem be the way it was, the way it had to be. I read a comment by a Swedish reader who had first read and loved an earlier, Swedish edition, when the poem was still divided into sections. She said that when she read the final version, she started feeling uncomfortable and then almost mad at me. Because I'd changed the game, and she liked it the way it had been before: it had a structure. And then, she wrote, she suddenly got it: she suddenly understood what the poem was really about. She let herself forget how good she felt with all that structure and let herself flow with the poem—and then she got it. I think that's the heart of the poem.

MS: In earlier editions of the poem, you collaborated with visual artists. How do you understand your relationship with visual artists and the relationship of your poetry with the visual world?

GG: I am a very visual person with a very strong sense of aesthetics; the world enters me through my eyes: light, colors, forms, objects, landscapes. Some of the things I like most are fashion, movies, and binge-watching TV series! So, at times I impart this visual quality to the poem. The way I place the text on the page has much to do with that visual sense. I also think of the book as a visual object.

MS: You started writing what would become *Migraciones* when you were in your early thirties. At that point you were reading voraciously and starting to write a lot, as well. Then you and the poem grew. I'm thinking of three archetypal figures or voices in the poem—the daughter, the mother, and the grandmother—and how, chronologically speaking, you're now the age of the grand-mother. You're the elder now, looking back. What are your thoughts about that progression in your life, in relation to the archetypal figures of the poem?

GG: I haven't thought too much about it. It doesn't matter what age you are; you continue being all the personae that are you. I now may be more the child because I'm entering a new stage in my life, like a child. I don't know what old age will be, so I'm entering old age with no knowledge. It's like you becoming a father. You didn't know how to be a father, so you were like a newborn father. I think that I'm now in a transition, a very strange and difficult transition in my life. I almost really gave birth to the poem: pushed it out, pushed him out of me, and now we're two different entities. I'm still backing him up, like helping with the translations and giving readings. I'm backing him up, because I will always be his mother. But now he's a forty-four-year-old big boy, and he has to go out into the world. With or without me.

You never really know what you wrote: why, where it's going, how good it is. I can just tell you that I did my very, very best. I can also tell you that the poem is finished. It had to finish. I closed the door. And since I really closed it, I know the poem also sort of said, "Okay, this is where we part."

MS: This is my last question: Do you think the reader of your poetry has any responsibility reading it? Is anything required of the reader?

GG: The book is there; it's a closed thing, sheets of paper with words on them. And the reader is what gives it life. I think that the most important thing the poet can do is to dare to write, and for the reader, to allow himself or herself to be carried away. The book is full of questions, and I don't think that the important thing is to have the answers. Perhaps, even more than in the anecdotal part about these Jewish women, it's in all these questions that give way to more questions, which are answered by still other questions, that the Jewishness of the poem lies.

Really, poetry is nothing but a mouthful of air, nothing but words. But these words transform the human heart and open you to the immensity of life. Reading a Chinese poet, you may end up traveling much farther than if you actually went to see the Great Wall of China. Probably you'd get there, and people would be taking pictures, talking, all kinds of things would be going on, and you wouldn't even be looking at the Wall. In my experience, the farthest you can go is almost always through poetry. Certainly, there are other paths, other ways. This is the one that I chose—without even knowing I was choosing it. I don't have an answer. I have questions that lead to more questions. Poetry is the gift, but it's a gift that requires that you give it to others.

NOTES

1. Gloria Gervitz, *Migraciones*, selection and prologue by Raúl Dorra and Blanca Alberta Rodríguez (Morelia, Michoacán, Mexico: Red Utopía, A.C./*jitanjáfora* Morelia, 2003), xv–xvi.

2. Andrea Castro, host, "Especial de Gloria Gervitz," *Poesía al paso* podcast, episode 5, March 21, 2017, https://poesiaalpasopodcast.word-press.com/2017/03/21/episodio-5-especial-de-gloria-gervitz/.

3. Diego José, "Gloria Gervitz y 'Migraciones': el poema de una vida," *Milenio*, July 26, 2019, https://www.milenio.com/cultura/laberinto/llevo-42-anos-conviviendo-poema-gloria-gervitz.

4. Lao Tzu, Tao Te Ching, trans. David Hinton (New York: Counterpoint Press, 2000), ix.

5. Pages 111–112, 114–116, 143, 153, and 161, along with the first four lines of page 110, the last four lines of page 113, and all but the last two words of page 117 are in English in the original Spanish text of *Migraciones*.

6. Nicolás López Pérez, "'Migraciones', de Gloria Gervitz: El milagro de la herida," Cine y Literatura, May 7, 2020, https://www.cineyliteratura.cl/migraciones-de-gloria-gervitz-el-milagro-de-la-herida/.

7. Translation by Mark Schafer of the original poem (received via private email correspondence):

DE IR A POLONIA

¿a dónde es que regreso al venir aquí?

¿dónde duelen estas raíces?

de aquí salí de aquí partí aún antes de nacer,

y aquí regreso nacida,
aquí regreso temblando,

aquí para mirar con mis ojos lo que miraron mis padres,
mis abuelos, los bisabuelos, generaciones perdidas en el tiempo,

regreso a lo olvidado,
regreso para recordar todo ese olvido,
regreso para decir Kadish por todos los que aquí quedaron,
regreso para decir Kadish por mí

8. Rose S. Minc, "'Fragmento de ventana': hacia una hagiografía de las olvidadas," *Folio*, no. 17, ed. Judith Morganroth Schneider (September 1987): 122–126.

TRANSLATOR'S ACKNOWLEDGMENTS

I WISH TO EXPRESS my deep gratitude and appreciation to Forrest Gander and Tony Frazier for championing *Migraciones* in the English-speaking world and for their unwavering support of my project to translate it into English. In 1993, when no other US editor would publish Gloria's work, Forrest Gander included selections from her poem (in Stephen Tapscott's translation) in his landmark anthology *Mouth to Mouth: Poems by Twelve Contemporary Mexican Women*. Ten years later, when still no US editor would publish Gervitz's work, Tony Frazier, editor and publisher of Shearsman Books (UK), proclaimed the need for *Migrations* to be published in English, sought out my translation, and then published it himself in a gorgeous edition the following year (followed soon after by Junction Press in the US). I celebrate this final edition with the two of you.

I also want to thank Gloria, for letting me accompany her on this extraordinary journey through thirty years of her writing life and for accompanying and assisting me throughout. She patiently and carefully answered all of my questions, over many years, and reviewed and critiqued many of my draft translations, from the early 1990s through the early 2020s. While I take full and sole responsibility for the English translation, Gloria's feedback enriched and informs the poem you now hold in your hands.

—Mark Schafer
Roxbury, Massachusetts
June 2021

DANTE ALIGHIERI The New Life
Translated by Dante Gabriel Rossetti; Preface by Michael Palmer

KINGSLEY AMIS Collected Poems: 1944–1979

GUILLAUME APOLLINAIRE Zone: Selected Poems
Translated by Ron Padgett

AUSTERITY MEASURES The New Greek Poetry
Edited by Karen Van Dyck

SZILÁRD BORBÉLY Berlin-Hamlet
Translated by Ottilie Mulzet

ANDRÉ BRETON AND PHILIPPE SOUPAULT The Magnetic Fields
Translated by Charlotte Mandel

MARGARET CAVENDISH *Edited by Michael Robbins*

NAJWAN DARWISH Exhausted on the Cross
Translated by Kareem James Abu-Zeid; Foreword by Raúl Zurita

BENJAMIN FONDANE Cinepoems and Others
Edited by Leonard Schwartz

PERE GIMFERRER *Translated by Adrian Nathan West*

SAKUTARŌ HAGIWARA Cat Town
Translated by Hiroaki Sato

MICHAEL HELLER Telescope: Selected Poems

MIGUEL HERNÁNDEZ *Selected and translated by Don Share*

RICHARD HOWARD RH ♥ HJ and Other American Writers
Introduction by Timothy Donnelly

LOUISE LABÉ Love Sonnets and Elegies
Translated by Richard Sieburth

CLAIRE MALROUX Daybreak: New and Selected Poems
Translated by Marilyn Hacker

ARVIND KRISHNA MEHROTRA *Selected by Vidyan Ravinthiran;
Introduction by Amit Chaudhuri*

HENRI MICHAUX A Certain Plume
Translated by Richard Sieburth; Preface by Lawrence Durrell

MELISSA MONROE Medusa Beach and Other Poems

JOAN MURRAY Drafts, Fragments, and Poems:
The Complete Poetry
Edited and with an introduction by Farnoosh Fathi; Preface by John Ashbery

SILVINA OCAMPO *Selected and translated by Jason Weiss*

EUGENE OSTASHEVSKY The Pirate Who Does Not Know
the Value of Pi
Art by Eugene and Anne Timerman

ELISE PARTRIDGE The If Borderlands: Collected Poems

VASKO POPA *Selected and translated by Charles Simic*

J.H. PRYNNE The White Stones
Introduction by Peter Gizzi

ALICE PAALEN RAHON Shapeshifter
Translated and with an introduction by Mary Ann Caws

A.K. RAMANUJAN The Interior Landscape: Classical Tamil
Love Poems

PIERRE REVERDY *Edited by Mary Ann Caws*

DENISE RILEY Say Something Back & Time Lived, Without
Its Flow

JACK SPICER After Lorca
Preface by Peter Gizzi

ALEXANDER VVEDENSKY An Invitation for Me to Think
Translated by Eugene Ostashevsky and Matvei Yankelevich

WALT WHITMAN Drum-Taps: The Complete 1865 Edition
Edited by Lawrence Kramer

ELIZABETH WILLIS Alive: New and Selected Poems

RAÚL ZURITA Inri
Translated by William Rowe; Preface by Norma Cole